WHAT'S WILDLIFE WORTH?

Economic contributions of wild plants and
animals to developing countries

Robert and Christine Prescott-Allen

An Earthscan Paperback

©Earthscan/PA DATA 1982
Reprinted 1985, 1986
ISBN 0-905347-35-8

Published by the International Institute for
Environment and Development, London and
Washington, DC

Printed by Russell Press Ltd, Nottingham, UK

Cover photo: The world's most widely
grown strains of high-yield rice gained
their disease-resistant characters from a
wild rice found in India. Indonesia: WHO
photo by P. Almasy.

What's wildlife worth?, edited and
produced by Jon Tinker, Barbara Cheney
and John McCormick, is based on research
by PA DATA for a joint programme of the
US Agency for International Development
and the US Man and the Biosphere
Program, funded through World Wildlife
Fund-US. It does not necessarily
represent the views of these or any other
organisations.

Earthscan is an editorially-independent
news and information service on global
development and environmental issues. The
book is part of an Earthscan programme on
wild genetic resources, funded by the
Swedish International Development
Authority. Part of the International
Institute for Environment and Development,
it is financially supported by several UN
agencies, the European Community, the
Nordic aid agencies (DANIDA, FINNIDA, NORAD
and SIDA), the Netherlands Foreign Ministry
and the World Bank.

This book is also available in Spanish.

CONTENTS

Executive Summary

> We depend on biosphere - coral and mangrove buffers
> - watersheds and erosion - Himalayan crisis - slash-
> and-burn - Altiplano and the Incas - pollination by
> midges - mangrove nurseries for shrimp - ecosupports
> are free goods

> Wildlife economically important - cultural role -
> value hard to quantify - what statisticians don't
> know - demand outstrips supply - habitat destruction
> - tomato, cocoa, wheat genes going - species safe
> but genes endangered - main conclusions - need for
> better figures - seed banks and nature reserves -
> integrate conservation with development - both North
> and South need Third World wildlife

Tropical forests are home to a wealth of biological diversity: perhaps half the species on the planet. They provide fuelwood, timber and wood products; concentrate nutrients into plants and animals of value to people; and play a vital ecological role in controlling flooding and soil erosion.

Brazil: FAO photo by Peyton Johnson

EXECUTIVE SUMMARY

This book aims to show that wild animals and plants make a big economic contribution to developing countries. It illustrates how that contribution is made, calls for a better evaluation of its value, and argues that if it is to be exploited sustainably, conservation must go hand in hand with development. . . . Page 10

Official UN figures claim that less than 1% of meat eaten in developing nations comes from wild game. This ignores game which is poached or goes straight into the pot. Some 7% of meat eaten in the Ivory Coast is wild - but the figure is 70% in the rain forest regions. . . . . Page 14

The crocodile skin trade has declined to one fifth its previous level, and the spotted cat trade shifted to smaller species as commerce in more endangered cats is banned. The price of rhino horn rose 25-fold in three years. But while poaching has pushed rhinos to the edge of extinction, the African elephant could still provide a sustainable yield of ivory. . . . . Page 17

Monkey meat sells for more than beef in Liberia, and in Nigeria meat from giant rats is three times the price of mutton. .Page 18

When fish are included, the totals are higher, especially in tropical Africa, southeast Asia, the Pacific and the Caribbean. The Maldive Islands get 93% of their fish and meat from the wild. Ghana, Congo and Sierra Leone get three quarters, Zaire, Indonesia and the two Koreas about two thirds. . . . . . .Page 21

Freshwater fish are widely eaten in Asia and Africa, especially where there are large lakes (Chad, Victoria, Tanganyika, Malawi) or in big rivers such as the Ganges, Irrawaddy, Mekong, Congo, Niger and Zambezi. .Page 21

In China much of the inland fisheries come from fish-farms, but elsewhere freshwater fish are almost entirely wild caught. Some

Wild animals have been little used in <u>livestock breeding.</u> An ibex has been crossed with a goat in Israel, and Chinese and Indian species of wild silkworms have been crossed in India. . . Page 64

<u>Using wild genes can be slow:</u> it will have taken 25 years before disease-resistant bananas are developed from wild trees. But in tomato, potato, peanut and cotton, wild genes are likely to be increasingly used. . . . . .Page 65

<u>Agriculture originated from wildlife.</u> Today, wildlife provides much of the genetic material for its repair and renewal. .Page 66

Coral and mangroves protect people and property from the sea, but these <u>ecosystems are frequently damaged.</u> And forests protect watersheds from erosion. Deforestation can cause siltation of reservoirs and harbours, loss of cropland, and massive flooding: the costs in India are over $1 billion a year. . . . . . .Page 67

Tropical forests, natural grasslands and marine plants in tropical estuaries all <u>concentrate nutrients</u> into plants and animals of value to people. . . . . Page 71

<u>Wild insects</u> pollinate some crops, and protect others from pests. . . . . .Page 72

Mangrove forests are valuable as <u>nurseries</u> for shrimp and fish. . . . . Page 73

Wildlife provides food, fuel, raw material, medicines, genes for plant breeders, and ecological buffering. Wildlife is also culturally valuable. .Page 76

The <u>economic benefits</u> are substantial, especially in the rural Third World, but often hard to quantify. . . . . .Page 77

Many wild resources are being damaged by <u>overexploitation</u> and by <u>habitat destruction.</u> At risk is valuable genetic material: wild olives in Algeria and Niger, wild tomatoes and cocoa in South America, wild bananas and sugarcane in SE Asia, wild wheat in West Asia and wild coffee in Africa. . . . . .Page 78

The book concludes that <u>wildlife is economically important</u> in the Third World; that it is easy to overlook and hard to evaluate; that it should be conserved and developed; and that genes may be at risk even where species are not. . . . . Page 80

Wild resources can be protected off-site in <u>gene banks</u>, zoos, farms etc; on-site in <u>reserves</u> (where new methods are needed to conserve genes as well as species); and by better resource management. . . . . Page 81

<u>Development is production</u>, and conservation is the maintenance of the means of production. The conservation and sutainable use of Third World wildlife contributes to the prosperity of all peoples, North and South. . . . . Page 82

Chapter One

INTRODUCTION

BEFORE THE INVENTION of agriculture, when human beings lived by hunting and gathering, people's dependence on the wild was absolute. Wild plants and animals were their only source of food, medicines, fuel and fibre.

Since the agricultural revolution the utilitarian importance of wildlife has clearly diminished. It might be assumed that today the contribution of wild living resources had become marginal to developed economies and will soon become so to developing ones.

Is this assumption correct? No. Evidence we have assembled for a report on the contribution of wild plants and animals to industrialised societies suggests that even today a significant proportion of economic activity remains dependent on wildlife.

Some uses of wildlife have persisted from paleolithic times: the hunting of marine fishes, for example. Other uses are new. For example, agricultural development needs wild plants as a source of genes for disease resistance. And wild organisms are used by the pharmaceutical industry as sources of valuable compounds that, once discovered in nature, can then be synthesised in the laboratory.

There has been no overall assessment of the importance of wild plants and animals to developing countries. A great many local studies have been made, and there are several excellent regional and sectoral reviews: those on the use of wild animals in West Africa (Ajayi 1979), on global use of firewood (Eckholm 1975) and on mangrove forests and fisheries (MacNae 1974) are examples. But for no country or region does there appear to have been a comprehensive analysis showing precisely the current economic contribution of wildlife: for the production of food, drugs and other essential raw materials; as an income earner; as a resource for genetic improvement of crops and livestock; and through the provision of ecological support for economic activity.

Without this type of information, politicians, government officials or others who make or influence decisions on resource management cannot evaluate the importance of wild plants and animals. So the ecosystems on which this wildlife depends are altered, often irreversibly, with little understanding of the social and economic consequences.

This report is not a comprehensive assessment. It is a review of reviews: a synthesis of the best available regional and sectoral studies. Its purpose is to show that wildlife does make a contribution to developing countries; to illustrate the ways that contribution is made; to show that the contribution is sufficiently important to justify more detailed and precise evaluation on a national or regional basis; and to indicate some key measures to conserve the resource and to integrate its conservation with development.

Wildlife can bring two types of economic benefit to developing peoples or countries. First, wildlife may be used directly as food, fodder, fuel or fibre. Second, that same wildlife may be sold, providing communities or countries with much-needed income. In some cases this income is a prominent item in national budgets; even where it is negligible in GNP terms, it is generally important and sometimes vital for the communities most closely concerned with the trade.

Wild plants and animals bring much needed income to a great many people in developing countries. Unhappy testimony to this is the fact that hundreds of species in trade are threatened, and many of those are seriously endangered. Even the species that are not threatened with extinction - most fisheries and timber trees - are subject to overexploitation: several major fish stocks have been depleted, and little if any logging is conducted sustainably.

Wild plants and animals of obvious value are subject to a management "Catch 22": if their economic utility is overlooked or ignored or if their use is in competition with some other human enterprise, they face the loss of the habitats on which they depend; if, however, their economic utility is evident, they are likely to be overexploited, often to economic extinction and sometimes to outright extinction. This is not a problem peculiar to developing countries; but its solution is one from which developing countries, particularly those that are poor in commodities, have most to gain.

Each country's physical resource base consists of living resources (such as fisheries, forests, farmland) and nonliving resources (such as minerals, petroleum, water). Living resources, either wild or domesticated, are renewable if conserved and destructible if not.

But most inventories and assessments blur the distinction between wild and domesticated living resources, if they make it at all. "Wildlife" may be regarded as referring only to game animals, or to all animals and plants that come under the jurisdiction of a particular government department.

This obscures a condition crucial to the conservation of all wild plants and animals: the need to maintain their habitats. Habitat conservation is a prerequisite for the sustainable development of wild living resources, whether commercial fisheries, industrial timber production, subsistence hunting and fishing, firewood collecting, or the gathering of medicinal herbs.

12

In this report we use the terms "wildlife", "wild plants and animals" and "wild living resources" interchangeably. Any of these phrases is employed to mean all wild plants (including fungi) and animals (mammals, birds, reptiles, amphibians, fishes and invertebrates). Logically they should also include microorganisms, but since the conservation of bacteria, viruses and moulds etc is rather different from that of larger organisms, we have not covered them in this report.

Conservation, like wildlife, is a word that can be defined in various ways and is easily misinterpreted. We follow the World Conservation Strategy's definition: "the management of human use of the biosphere (that is, all living things) so that it may yield the greatest sustainable benefit to present generations while maintaining its potential to meet the needs and aspirations of future generations" (IUCN 1980). So conservation includes preservation, sustainable use, enhancement and restoration. In short, conservation means maintenance.

Once conservation is recognised as maintenance of the means of development, then with forethought and care it becomes possible to integrate the two processes and hence to make development sustainable. Integration, however, depends first on recognition of the roles that ecosystems - and the wild, weed and domesticated species that comprise them - play in human economies. This report considers the role of those wild species reported to make a significant contribution to the economies of developing countries.

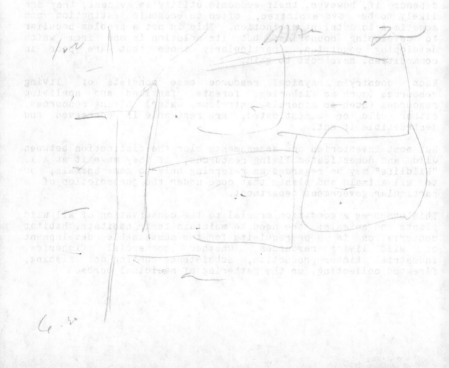

Chapter 2

MEAT, SKINS AND IVORY

THE CONTRIBUTION of wildlife to developing country diets is paradoxically both minor and vital. With the exception of the very few groups which still live by hunting and gathering (such as the San in Botswana) people now get their calories and staple foods from animals and plants that are domesticated. But the minor role of wildlife is still vital, because directly or indirectly wildlife supplies much of the animal protein consumed, as well as being a source of trace elements, nutritional variety, and from time to time famine relief.

Wildlife can provide welcome flavour, especially to poor diets dominated by starchy staples. An important use of fish (mostly anchovies) in southeast Asia, for example, is in the fish sauce known as Ngan-pyaye in Burma, Nam pla in Thailand, Tuk trey in Cambodia, Nam pa in Laos, and Nuoc mam in Vietnam. The sauce, made by salting and fermenting fish and then draining off the resulting liquid, is rich in B vitamins and protein and is an indispensable flavouring - the equivalent of soy sauce in Chinese and Japanese cooking (Brennan 1981; Davidson 1975).

If the available statistics are any guide, the contribution of game to meat production in developing countries is negligible. Figures for 1979 from the UN Food and Agriculture Organization (FAO) show that the developing countries' production of game meat was 450,000 tons (about the same as that of the developed countries a mere 0.9% of their total meat production of 47.89 million tons (mostly bovine and pork meats) (FAO 1980a).

But statistics are unreliable. Game kills are recorded only in countries with strictly enforced hunting regulations (such as the USA); other countries, including all developing countries, rely on estimates based on food consumption surveys - if they produce any statistics at all. Even when a country does issue estimates it may not include as game all wildlife consumed for meat. Frogs, lizards, turtles, snails, insects and other invertebrates may be added by FAO to meat from minor domesticated animals such as rabbits: FAO's statistics for this category show production by developing countries of 650,000 tons in 1979, or 1.4% (FAO 1980a).

Accurate data on wildlife consumption can be extraordinarily difficult to obtain. The sources of supply may be widely dispersed and there is often an incentive to conceal the catch, so as to avoid tax or conservation laws. And when the hunter sells the meat to a neighbour, or pops it into the family pot he rarely tells a statistician.

Even so, where people are poor, farm meat is expensive, and wild
animals are abundant enough to be killed without great
effort, wildlife is an important source of meat.

* In the Huallaga Central Region of Peru, new settlers and
  the indigenous communities get as much as 80% of their
  animal protein from wildlife (AID 1979, cited in Library
  of Congress 1979d).

* In the Ucayli region of Peru, wildlife supplies about 85%
  of the animal protein consumed in rural areas (de Vos
  1977).

* Elsewhere in the Amazon basin reported consumption is
  much lower: from 20% down to 2% along Brazil's Trans-
  amazon Highway (Smith 1976, cited in de Vos 1977). The
  lower percentages reflect a decline in supply rather
  than a decline in demand.

The figures suggest that Latin America, and Asia plus the
Pacific, each account for about 9% of game meat output by
developing countries. The remaining 82% comes from Africa (FAO
1980a). Not surprisingly, the best surveys on consumption of game
meat have been made in Africa, and have been summarised by de Vos
(1977), Sale (unpublished) and, for West Africa only, Ajayi
(1979).

Figure 1 shows the estimated annual output of game meat in
Africa. In only 11 of the 23 countries does game meat contribute
10% or more to the per capita supply of animal protein; and in
only two does it supply more than 20%.

But other surveys show that in some parts of these countries the
contributions of wild land animals to animal protein consumption
is much higher.

According to Ajayi (1979), forest wildlife supplies 20% of the
annual consumption of animal protein among rural people living in
Nigeria's tropical rain forest (trf) zone, compared with 13% for
the whole country. Among rural people in the trf zone of the
Ivory Coast the figure is 70% compared with 7.4% for the whole
country. And in Cameroon's trf zone it is 70-80% compared with
2.8% for the whole country.

The national average contribution of bushmeat to animal protein
in Ghana is only 9.2% nationally. But in the Asempaneye and
Wiawso Districts it is 31% and 44% respectively (Asibey 1978,
cited in Ajayi 1979); and in other rural districts of Ghana as
much as 73% of the meat eaten comes from the wild (Asibey 1974).

Some of the higher figures may be due to an overenthusiastic
advocacy of the value of game. Ajayi's claim that forest wildlife
supplies 80-90% of Liberia's animal protein (Ajayi 1979) is
difficult to reconcile with FAO figures indicating that 50% of

Figure 1. Estimated annual game output and per capita supply in selected African countries.

	Output 000 metric tons		Supply per capita kg		Contribution of game meat to per capita animal protein supply
	1972-74	1977	1972-74	1977	%
Angola	6	6	1.0	0.9	4.5
Benin	6	6	2.2	1.9	13.2
Botswana	5	6	7.6	7.5	15.8
Cameroon	4	4	0.6	0.6	2.8
Chad	3	3	0.8	0.7	3.2
Congo	5	6	4.0	4.0	16.9
Ethiopia	7	7	0.2	0.2	1.0
Gambia	1	1	1.7	1.8	7.8
Ghana	26	28	2.8	2.7	9.2
Guinea	4	4	0.9	0.8	10.0
Ivory Coast	13	13	2.8	2.5	7.4
Kenya	7	7	0.6	0.5	2.6
Lesotho	3	4	3.0	2.9	13.4
Liberia	5	5	2.8	3.0	15.2
Namibia	2	2	2.6	2.6	3.9
Nigeria	87	95	1.2	1.2	13.0
Rwanda	5	6	1.3	1.3	25.0
Sudan	6	7	0.4	0.3	1.0
Tanzania	7	8	0.5	0.5	1.6
Togo	4	4	1.9	1.7	13.2
Uganda	12	14	1.1	1.2	5.0
Zaire	90	68	3.9	2.6	26.8
Zambia	17	20	3.7	3.7	13.4

Sources: 1972-74 mean: FAO 1977a; 1977: FAO Interlinked Computer System, cited by Krostitz 1979

Liberia's animal protein comes from fish (FAO 1977a). Nicol (1953) reported that the Isoko farmers of the Niger delta in Nigeria obtain 12 grams of protein per day from fish, 1 gram from livestock (goats), and 7.2 grams from game (mostly monkeys, but also pangolin, porcupine, grasscutter and giant rats, snails, frogs and palm weevils). De Vos (1977) summarises this as follows: "The Isoko tribe (Niger delta) obtain 20g/day of animal protein, mainly game". (20 grams is 0.7 ounces.)

These discrepancies may also be terminological. While "game" usually means wild land animals, its meaning can be extended to include fish and other wild aquatic animals as well. But the main reason for the great variation in figures on the importance of game is probably an equally great variation in the facts. Butynski and von Richter (1974) write of Botswana that "the proportion of wild to domestic animal meat in people's diets varies within the country. For instance, all the meat eaten by Bushmen (San) is game, while cattle-raising tribesmen get about 80% of their meat from wildlife and 20% from their livestock. People living in or close to villages tend to eat a higher proportion of meat from cattle, goats and sheep, but their main supply still comes from game animals".

Although the picture is blurred and incomplete, it is clear that large numbers of people - particularly in Africa - depend on wild land animals for a significant proportion of their animal protein.

* In Ghana about three quarters of the population is heavily dependent on wildlife for protein (Asibey 1974).

* In southern Nigeria game meat is eaten regularly by about 80% of the population. The annual value of wild meat (including fish) consumed in 1965/66 has been estimated at US$20.4 million, compared with $34 million for domestic animal meat (Ajayi 1979).

* In Liberia, 70% of the rural population is said to eat some bushmeat, or to make money by selling bushmeat (Library of Congress, 1980d).

The most important food animals are the smaller ones that flourish in secondary growth. An analysis of market records in Ghana reveals that giant rats (mostly grasscutters Thryonomys species) dominate the take; followed by small antelopes such as grey duiker (Sylvicapra grimmia), bushbuck (Tragelaphus scriptus), royal antelope (Neotragus pygmaeus) and black duiker (Cephalophus niger); and monkeys such as the green monkey (Cercopithecus aethiops) (Asibey 1974). Duikers and monkeys are also the main source of wild animal protein in Zaire (Heymans & Maurice 1973, cited in de Vos 1977).

De Vos (1977) attributes the emphasis on rodents and other small game to three factors. They are not covered by game laws and so can be taken without restriction; they have a higher reproductive rate and hence a higher sustainable yield than larger species; they are more numerous than the bigger animals in areas of high human population density.

The consumption figures show a predominance of animals that do relatively well in ecologically degraded conditions. This suggests that without good management the contribution of wild land animals to the African diet will decline.

Species adapted to a combination of primary and secondary ecosystems (eg virgin forest) are becoming less available, and animals adapted only to successional ecosystems (eg secondary scrub) are easier to catch. Another sign of this shift is the high cost of bushmeat. Figure 2 shows that a kilogram of meat from some, theoretically abundant, species can cost more than twice as much as beef, pork or mutton.

Wild animals enter the economy in a number of other ways than as food: either dead (in the form of hides, furs and other skins, ivory, ornaments and souvenirs) or alive (for the pet trade, for biomedical research, and for zoos).

Wild skins come mainly from reptiles in Asia and South America. Bangladesh, Indonesia, Malaysia, Pakistan and the Philippines are the major Asian suppliers of lizard skins, especially from monitor lizards (Varanus).

Indonesia, the Philippines and Thailand are the main suppliers of snakeskins. Until 1976, when the export of raw snakeskin was banned, India was also a prominent source, selling as many as three million snakeskins a year. Snake and lizard are the main types of wild skin sold by Asian countries, while South America, especially Colombia, Panama and Paraguay, exports mostly the skins of crocodiles and lizards (Inskipp and Wells 1979).

The crocodile skin trade has declined from 5-10 million hides a year in the 1950s and early 1960s to some two million a year today. The main reasons for the decline are the growing costs of the skilled labour required to make quality crocodile leather products and the scarcity of the raw material (King 1978).

The choice American species, the American crocodile (Crocodylus acutus) and the Orinoco crocodile (C. intermedius) are critically endangered as a result of overexploitation. The second-choice species, the black caiman (Melanosuchus niger) and the broadsnouted caiman (Caiman latirostris), are virtually extinct, also because of excessive hunting for hides. The trade has therefore had to turn to inferior American types, besides continuing to take the smaller quantities of high quality Asian and African crocodile skins (notably those of the saltwater crocodile (Crocodylus porosus) that still come on the market (IUCN 1979; King 1978).

Trade in wild furs is much smaller than that in reptile skins. Trade in spotted cats makes up less than 1% of the number of furs in commerce, but accounts for more than 8% of earnings. Many of the species - for example, jaguar (Panthera onca) and cheetah (Acinonyx jubatus) - are so at risk that they are on Appendix I of the Convention on International Trade in Endangered Species of Wild Fauna and Flora (CITES). Trade in Appendix I species is prohibited; trade in Appendix II species is regulated.

The industry has responded by putting more pressure on the smaller cats. About 60% of the 1977 trade originated in Central and South America, consisting mostly of ocelot (Felis pardalis:

Figure 2. Comparison of prices of game meat and livestock meat (in US dollars per kilogram) in selected West African cities (Ajayi,1979).

	Accra, Ghana	Ibadan, Nigeria	Sabouang, Cameroon	Abidjan, Ivory Coast	Monrovia, Liberia
	1970	1975	1978	1978	1979
Game meat					
hares (1)	-	7.20	3.75	-	-
brushtailed porcupine (2)	1.06	-	4.37	-	2.50
African giant rat (3)	0.51	5.00	-	-	-
grasscutter (4)	1.06	9.60	-	10.00	1.00
duikers (5)	-	-	2.50	-	-
grey duiker (6)	0.88	6.80	-	-	4.00
bay duiker (7)	0.86	-	-	-	-
black duiker (8)	0.79	5.20	-	-	-
bushbuck (9)	0.66	5.20	-	-	-
monkeys (10)	-	-	3.75	-	-
green monkey (11)	0.79	-	-	-	-
spotnose monkey (12)	-	-	-	-	2.50
red colobus (13)	-	-	-	-	3.00
mangabeys (14)	-	-	-	-	3.00
Livestock meat					
beef	0.30-0.45	4.20	2.50	3.00	2.50
pork	-	4.40	2.00	6.00	2.50
mutton	0.61	2.80	3.50	3.50	2.00

Scientific names: (1) Lepus, (2) Atherurus africanus, (3) Cricetomys gambianus, (4) Thrynomys swinderianus, (5) Cephalophus, (6) Sylvicapra grimmia, (7) Cephalophus dorsalis, (8) C.niger, (9) Tragelaphus scriptus, (10) Cercopithecus, (11) C.aethiops, (12) C.ascanius, (13) Colobus badius, (14) Cercocebus.

31,700 pelts), margay (Felis wiedii: 30,000), tigercat (Felis tigrina: 14,600), and Geoffroy's cat (Felis geoffroyi: 13,000). Much of this, since it dealt heavily in several endangered species, was illegal (Inskipp and Wells 1979).

South America is also a prominent source of less valuable skins from wild animals that are not threatened, among them the collared peccary (Tayassu tajacu), whitelipped peccary (T. pecari) and brocket deer (Mazama species). Between 1962 and 1972 Peru exported more than 2.3 million peccary skins and more than 300,000 brocket deer skins (Smith 1978).

Wild animals also supply a host of special products - special in the sense that they have intrinsic value and thus are likely to have buyers irrespective of the availability of substitutes. The horns of rhinos are greatly prized in West Asia where they are made into ornate dagger handles. They are also valued for carving in East Asia, where powdered rhino horn is used in medicine.

It is now believed that the horn's reputed power as a sexual stimulant is not the cause of the rhino's demise, since the powder comes from the waste from carvings. The demand for the horn as an ornament is very much greater. The price has risen dramatically - from $27 a kilogram in 1975 to $675 a kilogram in 1978 ($12-309 per pound)- with disastrous consequences for the survival of all five rhino species (Inskipp and Wells 1979).

Another intrinsically valuable ornamental product from the wild is tortoiseshell, the carapace of the hawksbill turtle (Eretmochelys imbricata). During the period 1930-1945 it was thought that tortoiseshell had been replaced by plastic imitations, but after World War II the market recovered as people realized that the particular beauty of genuine tortoiseshell could not be imitated. Now more than 90 tons are traded annually, half of it from Indonesia and Thailand, the rest from more than two dozen countries of the Pacific, the Indian Ocean and the Caribbean (Inskipp and Wells 1979).

Elephant ivory is perhaps the most famous of the intrinsically valuable wild animal products. Used as an ornament, it has recently acquired importance as a hedge against inflation. Like rhino horn, its value soared from $7-25 a kilogram in the 1960s to $110 a kilogram in the mid-1970s (from $3-11 to $50 per pound) (Inskipp and Wells 1979; Ricciuti 1980).

At the same time exports from Africa also rose sharply. During 1971, for example, Kenya's ivory exports jumped by 86% over the previous year, and then in 1972 by another 81% (Ricciuti 1980). Many African elephant populations suffer heavily from poaching as well as legal ivory hunting.

The main ivory suppliers at present are probably Zaire, Central African Republic, Uganda, Kenya, Tanzania, Sudan, Congo and South

20

Africa. Most of the ivory ends up in East Asia, particularly
Japan and Hong Kong, which in 1978 alone imported almost 1,000 t
(Inskipp and Wells 1979). Unlike the rhinos, the African elephant
is not yet in danger of extinction. Theoretically, therefore, it
should be possible for the ivory trade to continue, as a
valuable source of revenue for the African countries concerned.
This should be a sufficient incentive for them to regulate the
trade at sustainable levels.

WILD LAND ANIMALS in developing country diets are generally used to supplement the bigger contributions of livestock (including eggs and dairy products) and of fish and other wild aquatic animals. Indeed when the figures for aquatic animals are added to those of the land, the number of countries with a substantial dependence on wildlife for animal protein increases dramatically.

Figure 3 lists 62 countries obtaining 20% or more of their average daily per capita supply of animal protein from wild animals. Of these, 19 obtain 50% or more. The Maldive Islands in the Indian Ocean obtain 93% of their animal protein from the wild; Ghana, Congo and Sierra Leone about three quarters; and Zaire, Liberia, Indonesia and the two Koreas about two thirds.

Outside Africa, land animals seem to make an important contribution to nutrition in only one of the countries listed: Papua New Guinea. There, wild sources supply 60% of the daily per capita animal protein supply - 18.2 grams (0.64 ounces). (Wild sources: marine animals 7.9 grams, land animals 2.6 grams, and freshwater animals 0.4 grams; domesticated sources: meat 6.4 grams, milk products 0.7 grams, and eggs 0.2 grams).

Freshwater species supply 10% or more of the per capita animal protein intake in 16 countries and 20% or more in 13 countries - all in Asia or Africa.

* Some of these countries have major lake fisheries: Chad, Malawi, Tanzania, Uganda.

* Others have large river systems, such as the Ganga-Brahmaputra (Bangladesh), Irrawaddy (Burma), Mekong (Laos, Cambodia, Thailand), Congo (Congo, Zaire), Niger (Mali), and Zambezi (Zambia).

* Benin and a few others get much of their freshwater fish from lagoons, where yields are increased by planting brushwood, so expanding the surface area for growth of the periphyton (small water plants and algae) on which the fish feed. Under simple management such as this, these "fish parks" yield as much as 8,000 kilograms/hectare/year (7,100 pounds/acre) of tilapia and other fish species (Lowe-McConnell 1977).

The annual freshwater catch in Asia has averaged more than four and a quarter million metric tons in the five years since 1975 - well over the total catch of almost three million metric tons for the rest of the world's inland waters. The second largest annual

Figure 3. Daily per capita supply of animal protein from the wild
(in grams) in 62 countries (Source: FAO 1977a).These countries
lie within two large and two small wild animal protein zones. The
two large zones are the African (from Cape Verde and Mauritania
in the west to Tanzania and the Comoros in the east), and the
Asian-Pacific zone (from Bangladesh through Southeast Asia and
the Pacific islands to Samoa and Tahiti). The two small zones are
the Caribbean and the Western Indian Ocean (Sri Lanka, Yemen and
the islands).

	total animal products	"game meat"	"fish & seafood"	total wild meat	wild as % of total
Africa					
Angola	11.0	0.5	3.8	4.3	39.1
*Benin	8.3	1.1	3.7	4.8	57.8
Cameroon	10.7	0.3	3.8	4.1	38.3
Cape Verde	6.6	-	2.8	2.8	42.4
Chad	12.4	0.4	4.5	4.9	39.5
Comoros	6.6	-	1.9	1.9	28.8
*Congo	11.8	2.0	6.9	8.9	75.4
Gambia	11.5	0.9	3.8	4.7	40.9
*Ghana	15.2	1.4	10.0	11.4	75.0
Guinea	4.0	0.4	0.8	1.2	30.0
Ivory Coast	18.8	1.4	7.7	9.1	48.4
*Liberia	9.2	1.4	4.6	6.0	65.2
Malawi	5.6	-	2.5	2.5	44.6
Mali	9.2	-	2.5	2.5	27.2
Mauritania	31.6	-	6.9	6.9	21.8
Nigeria	4.6	0.6	0.8	1.4	30.4
Rwanda	2.8	0.7	0.1	0.8	28.6
Sao Tome	8.6	-	4.1	4.1	47.7
*Senegal	17.1	-	9.6	9.6	56.1
*Sierra Leone	10.0	0.3	7.2	7.5	75.0
Tanzania	12.8	0.2	3.3	3.5	27.3
*Togo	6.8	0.9	3.1	4.0	58.8
Uganda	11.9	0.6	4.7	5.3	44.5
*Zaire	7.1	1.9	2.6	4.5	63.4
Zambia	13.4	1.8	3.9	5.7	42.5
Asia & the Pacific					
*Bangladesh	6.7	-	3.5	3.5	52.2
Brunei	30.6	-	10.9	10.9	35.6
Burma	8.8	-	4.0	4.0	45.4
French Polynesia	33.4	0.2	11.4	11.6	34.7

	total animal products	"game meat"	"fish & seafood"	total wild meat	wild as % of total
Hong Kong	44.4	-	14.8	14.8	33.3
*Indonesia	5.3	-	3.6	3.6	67.9
Kampuchea (Cambodia)	7.5	-	3.2	3.2	42.7
*Korea DPR (North)	12.1	-	8.0	8.0	66.1
*Korea Rep (South)	13.1	-	9.0	9.0	68.7
Laos	9.5	-	1.9	1.9	20.0
Macau	31.2	-	8.1	8.1	26.0
*Malaysia, Sabah	22.1	-	11.3	11.3	51.1
*Malaysia, Sarawak	15.5	-	9.3	9.3	60.0
New Hebrides	34.7	-	11.1	11.1	32.0
*Papua New Guinea	18.2	2.6	8.3	10.9	59.9
*Philippines	16.9	-	8.9	8.9	52.7
Samoa	21.6	-	7.5	7.5	34.7
Singapore	37.6	-	13.7	13.7	36.4
Solomon Islands	11.4	-	4.6	4.6	40.3
*Thailand	13.2	-	6.8	6.8	51.5
*Vietnam	14.0	-	7.8	7.8	55.7

Caribbean

Antigua	31.6	-	8.6	8.6	27.2
Dominica	26.6	-	7.5	7.5	28.2
Fiji	19.3	-	7.0	7.0	36.3
Grenada	27.1	-	11.5	11.5	42.4
Guadeloupe	31.9	-	9.2	9.2	28.8
Guyana	21.6	-	5.8	5.8	26.8
Jamaica	30.8	-	8.4	8.4	27.3
Martinique	37.8	-	11.1	11.1	29.4
St.Lucia	29.7	-	9.5	9.5	32.0
St.Vincent	24.0	-	5.7	5.7	23.7
Suriname	20.7	-	6.6	6.6	31.9

Western Indian Ocean

*Maldives	30.6	-	28.4	28.4	92.8
Mauritius	15.7	-	4.9	4.9	31.2
Reunion	29.3	-	6.5	6.5	22.2
Sri Lanka	6.6	-	2.6	2.6	39.4
Yemen PDR	13.8	-	5.6	5.6	40.6

*Countries which obtain 50% or more of their average daily per capita supply of animal protein from the wild.

average freshwater catch - that of Africa - is just under one and a half million metric tons and is as great as that of Europe and all the Americas combined.

A proportion of these catches, however, comes from aquaculture. China alone accounts for more than a million tons of the Asian inland catch, and much of this comes from aquaculture in the strict sense of the term: the cultivation of aquatic organisms throughout their life cycles rather than simply giving wild seed or fry assistance at a certain stage in the cycle. Although pond culture is important elsewhere in South and East Asia (and to a much lesser extent in Africa), it is fair to say that outside China wild and semiwild species still dominate the freshwater catch (FAO 1980b; Tapiador et al 1977).

About 60% of the recorded landings in Africa come from the major lakes (such as Chad, Victoria, Tanganyika and Malawi), the remainder coming from the floodplains and lower reaches of the larger rivers. As with so much wildlife use, however, what is recorded represents only a part of what is taken. Much of the riverine catch comes, unremarked by the statisticians, from the continent's numerous smaller streams, providing communities isolated from other sources of fish with one of their few sources of animal protein (Welcomme 1974).

The floodplain fisheries of African rivers such as the Kafue in Zambia, the Niger in Mali and the Ouémé in Benin are a means of providing animal protein that can be integrated with wildlife production on land or with pastoralism. If left wild, the plain is colonised during the dry season with grasses that support game animals such as hippopotamus.

Under pastoralism the same grasses support herds of cattle, and many traditional nomadic cycles have been based on floodplains, such as the inland delta of the Niger and the Sudd of the Nile. Under either regime, dung from the animals returns nutrients to the system, which go to sustain the populations of fishes that invade the plain during the flood.

In Asia the mainstay of the freshwater fisheries is the rivers; but a vast network of lesser waterways - flooded rice paddies, swamps, ditches, canals and ponds - also makes an important contribution. In Thailand more than 60% of the rural people depend on fish as their main source of animal protein, catching it with baskets, fences, nets, rods and traps (Brennan 1981). The most widely consumed fishes are the carp-like species and the catfishes; in Laos at least 30 of the former and 20 of the latter are regularly brought to market (Davidson 1975).

Most of the countries listed in Figure 3 get the bulk of their wild animal protein from the fishes, crustaceans and molluscs of the sea. The small island nations, such as the Maldives, Cape Verde, Grenada and Fiji, obtain all of their wild animal protein from the sea. But the sea is also the main source in countries like Guyana, Yemen and the two Koreas, and in southeast Asia,

Many developing nations obtain the bulk of their protein from wild fish. So great is the demand for seafood for domestic consumption and for export that many fisheries are being severely overexploited.

Brazil: UN photo

Most developing countries earning substantial revenues from fishing get their catches from within 200 nautical miles of their coasts. South Korea has a large fishing fleet operating far from home waters, but its exports are being reduced as access to fishing areas is restricted.

South Korea: UN photo by M. Guthrie

where exploitation of marine living resources is still largely by traditional methods, although modern fishing vessels, nets and fish location technologies are having an increasing impact. In fact so great is the demand for seafood, for domestic consumption and for export, that the heavy concentration in inshore waters of old and new fisheries is having a disastrous impact on several stocks.

The most important pelagic (free-swimming) species in the region are mackerel (Rastrelliger), Spanish mackerel (Scomberomorus), round scad (Decapterus), sardines (Sardinella) and anchovies (mostly Stolephorus). Except in the Philippines, which uses modern purse seiners, these species are caught largely by traditional gear such as locally made seines, drift and gillnets, liftnets and traps (Kume 1973; Menasveta et al 1973).

The demersal (bottom) fishery is more at risk, since it has adopted more modern gear and techniques. In the early 1970s, when only Singapore and the Philippines had modern purse seines, all countries in the region (with the exception of Singapore) had modern trawls (Aoyama 1973). Unfortunately, motorised vessels with modern gear, rather than exploiting new offshore areas, have tended to fish the very inshore areas to which the traditional fishermen are confined. The result has been overfishing together with an increasing proportion of undersized juveniles in the catches, since greater fishing effort has been concentrated on the nursery area of many of the bottom-living species (Aoyama 1973; Anon 1981).

Overexploitation, of course, is not confined to marine wildlife but extends also to the wild resources of fresh waters and the land. Apart from anything else, it is a demonstration of the enormous popularity of wild fish, flesh and fowl.

Fisheries dominate the trade in wild animals. In the five-year period 1974-1978, the average annual value of developing country fishery exports was $3.2 billion (FAO 1980d), second only to timber at $4.5 billion. During that period 28 developing countries received an average of $10 million a year or more from the export of fisheries products.

As Figure 4 also shows, seven of those countries earned an average of more than $100 million a year, and for three of them (Panama, Peru and Senegal) exports of fisheries products provided 10% or more of their total export income. For a number of the countries listed the importance of fisheries is greater than these figures suggest. In Bangladesh, for example, where fisheries exports make up 3% of total export income, fishing is, after agriculture, the second most important economic activity (Library of Congress 1980a).

The international fishery trade has recently been strongly influenced by the widespread declaration of Exclusive Economic Zones (EEZs) or fishery zones for 200 nautical miles (371 kilometres) offshore. Foreign fleets have been limited by new catch quotas, have had to negotiate licences to fish, or have been forced to move elsewhere.

This has not been much of a problem for developing countries, although South Korea has suffered a reduction in exports (for example, by 19% between 1976 and 1977) as access to fishing areas has been restricted. Many developing countries have benefitted greatly, by gaining jurisdiction over major fisheries, among them Mauritania, Morocco and Senegal; Bangladesh, China and Vietnam; and Mexico, Chile and Peru (FAO 1978a; FAO 1978b).

Figure 4. Developing countries with fishery commodity exports greater than $10 million per year (FAO 1980d).

	Average annual exports of fishery commodities (1974-8) in thousands of US dollars	Percentage of total exports
Republic of Korea	443,537	5.5
Peru	231,838	16.4
India	176,811	3.3
Mexico	171,314	4.6
Thailand	150,869	4.9
Indonesia	119,261	1.3
Hong Kong	104,523	1.2
Chile	98,280	4.5
Malaysia	85,270	1.6
Morocco	76,773	5.2
Argentina	64,137	1.4
Brazil	60,097	0.6
Ecuador	56,840	4.7
Senegal	55,446	10.7
Panama	34,543	14.3
Philippines	33,992	1.2
Pakistan	33,921	3.0
Nicaragua	22,849	4.4
Papua New Guinea	20,518	3.3
Ivory Coast	17,488	1.0
Venezuela	17,430	0.2
Colombia	17,353	0.9
Turkey	15,614	0.9
Madagascar	15,074	4.9
Tunisia	12,875	1.4
Bangladesh	11,568	3.0
Honduras	11,464	2.8
Suriname	10,951	3.6

Morocco has been able to use its bigger bargaining power to persuade foreign countries to supply its processing plants with sardines caught in Moroccan waters, giving the nation a larger share of the profits of the fishery. Other countries can be expected to take similar steps, such as granting fishing rights in exchange for access to overseas markets - not only for fisheries products but also for other commodities (FAO 1978b).

Most developing countries earning substantial revenues from fishing, including Peru, India, Mexico and Indonesia, get their catches from within 200 nautical miles of their coasts. South Korea is unusual in that it has a large fleet operating far from home waters. South Korea is unusual in another respect too: its export catch is diverse, those of the other major countries depending on a single group of animals - anchoveta in the case of Peru and shrimp in the case of India, Mexico, Indonesia and Thailand.

Fish swimming in shoals, such as anchovies and sardinellas, make up a large part of the catches of several other countries, notably Morocco and the Ivory Coast; and shrimp are the main money earners for, among others, Panama, Pakistan and Madagascar.

Shrimp, in fact, are almost certainly the world's most valuable wild animals: the total annual value of developing country exports of fresh and frozen shrimp to developed countries is $1 billion - several hundred million dollars more than the next most lucrative export animals: cod and herring (FAO 1980b).

Not all fish are traded for food: tropical aquarium fishes are of growing importance. Demand for aquarium fish has increased since the 1960s at an average annual rate of 10-15%, and the annual values of the wholesale and retail trades are respectively $600 million and $1.5 billion.

Most of the freshwater species exported from southeast Asia are bred in captivity, but most freshwater species from elsewhere and virtually all marine species are captured from the wild: these represent 40-50% of all tropical aquarium fish sold.

South America is the biggest supplier of wild aquarium fish, followed by Asia (mostly the Philippines).

Chapter 4

VEGETABLES, SPICES AND CHEWING GUM

THE DIRECT CONTRIBUTION of wild plants to developing country diets is possibly less dramatic than that of wild animals. Indirectly it is at least as great and in many areas more so. This is because wild and semiwild plants are the major source of feed, fodder and forage for domesticated animals. As we will see in Chapter 8 (which covers indirect uses of wildlife), wild plants provide the ecological support for most of the animal protein that does not come directly from the wild.

The chief value of those wild plants consumed directly is in supplying trace elements, variety and a few extra vitamins. Wild plants are still the main source of leafy greens in many tropical areas where shifting cultivation (slash and burn) remains the principal means of food production. These greens are valuable suppliers of calcium, iron, ascorbic acid, and folic acid.

Wild greens also supply carotene or provitamin A, a nutrient which is particularly important in diets low in milk, eggs or liver. This is often the case with tropical subsistence diets composed largely of starchy staples. Xerophthalmia from vitamin A deficiency blinds 80,000 children a year (Oomen & Grubben 1978).

In any one area as many as 50-200 wild and weed species may be used from time to time as leaf vegetables. But very few are used regularly, and collectively it is unlikely they contribute more than 10% of the leaf vegetables actually consumed in areas of high population density (Grubben 1977; Oomen & Grubben 1978). This proportion may diminish further with urbanisation. Several wild plants continue to be useful complements of the cultivated ones, especially in Asia and Africa.

* The leaves of the baobab (Adansonia digitata), a wild and protected (even revered) tree of the African savannas, are used as a vegetable or in soups.

* Two aquatic weeds, kangkong (Ipomoea aquatica) and waterleaf (Talinum triangulare), are both cultivated and gathered from the wild, the former in southeast Asia, the latter in Brazil, West Africa and Indonesia.

* Crassocephalum biafrae, a climbing perennial, is unusual among tropical vegetables in that it flourishes in heavy shade: wild and cultivated plants of this species are eaten in southern Nigeria.

* Other wild plants that are commonly eaten (and also grown in home gardens occasionally) are a wild African eggplant

(Solanum aethiopicum), a strange southeast Asian shrub (Gnetum gnemon) with fleshy seeds, Gynandropsis gynandra in Africa, Pluchea indica in Indonesia, Malva species in Egypt and East Africa, and Spilanthes species in Central Africa and Indonesia (Grubben 1977; Oomen & Grubben 1978).

Most of these plants occur as weeds, thriving in hedgerows and secondary growth. Where they and similar species are used, it is a common practice for the cook simply to step outside and pluck whatever is readily to hand from the nearest patch of hedge or scrub.

Even more than the greens, the spices are of value in adding variety and interest to food rather than nutritive content. A number of wild spices enter trade, although they are generally regarded as inferior to their cultivated forms and fetch lower prices.

Allspice (Pimenta dioica) is an important cultivated crop in Jamaica, but also occurs in Mexico, Guatemala and Honduras, where the bulk of the crop is collected from wild trees. The market clearly distinguishes between Jamaican allspice, which is better in aroma, flavour and volatile-oil content, and Central American allspice. But Central American suppliers maintain their share of the market: roughly a third of the quantity and a quarter of the value of a trade worth some $6 million a year (Purseglove et al 1981a).

Cardamom (Elettaria cardamomum) is the third most expensive spice after saffron and vanilla. Until 1800 it came entirely from the wild, gathered from the evergreen monsoon forests of the Western Ghats in southern India and Sri Lanka. Now very little wild cardamom enters trade, but several cardamom substitutes come from the wild. The main ones, from related Elettaria, Amomum and Aframomum species, are:

* grains-of-paradise or melegueta pepper (Aframomum melegueta), sometimes cultivated but generally collected wild in West Africa;

* the bastard cardamom (Amomum xanthioides), which accounts for the greater part of Thailand's exports of "false cardamom";

* several other cardamom substitutes, mostly growing in South and East Asia, and traded within the region (Purseglove et al 1981b).

Another flavouring agent that comes largely from the wild is the tonka bean (Dipteryx odorata). It is abundant in northern South America; Venezuela is the biggest producer, selling the extract which is used for flavouring food and tobacco (Duke 1981).

Some roots also come from the wild: several wild yams (Dioscorea) are collected, particularly in times of food scarcity. Examples are D. lecardi in West Africa, D. luzonensis in the Philippines, and D. schimperiana in East and Central Africa (Coursey 1967).

The most important wild fruit is the mangosteen (Garcinia mangostana), claimed by many to be the most delicious of the tropical fruits, even "the finest fruit in the world". It grows wild in the tropical forests of Burma, Thailand, Cambodia, Vietnam, the Malay Peninsula and Indonesia (Sunda Islands and Moluccas). Although it is widely planted in Sri Lanka, the Philippines and India, most of the fruit marketed in the countries of its natural distribution are wild (Almeyda & Martin 1976).

Then there are <u>nuts</u>. The biggest selling wild nut species is the Brazil nut (Bertholletia excelsa), which forms large natural forests in the Amazon basin. Brazil is the major producer, and average annual output is more than 50,000 tons. But with the destruction of many of the country's Brazil nut stands and the development of other economic activities, commercial production is declining and supply cannot keep up with demand (USDA 1976; Woodroof 1979).

Pistachio is another nut of which apparently the world cannot have enough. Most of the commerical production comes from culti-vated Pistacia vera. Wild trees in Iran and Afghanistan, however, are also harvested and account for a useful proportion of the output of those countries (about 60,000 tons a year) (FAO 1980c; Maggs 1972).

Probably the two most important groups of food plants with species still harvested from the wild are the palms and the seaweeds.

* The wild palm Jessenia polycarpa is exploited in the Amazon regions of Colombia and northwestern Brazil for its seeds and edible oil. The oil is said to be comparable with that of olives (National Academy of Sciences 1979).

* Still more important sources of edible oil are the wild babassu palms, Orbignya oleifera and O. martiana from Brazil, and O. cuatrecasana from Colombia. The two Brazilian species occupy more than 35 million acres and supply local people not only with a readily accessible supply of cooking oil but also with oil for soap manufacture (National Academy of Sciences 1975).

* A number of wild Brazilian palm species - for example, Acrocomia, Euterpe, Prestoea, Roystonea, Sabal - are the major source of hearts of palm: the growing tips of palm trees which are eaten cooked or as a salad. Since the trees must be killed to obtain the hearts, long-overdue moves are being made to establish plantations (National Academy of Sciences 1975).

* Several wild as well as cultivated palm species produce an important subsistence staple: sago. Wild palms are used for sago in the eastern Orinoco delta in Venezuela (where the species are Mauritia flexuosa and Manicaria saccifera) and in Papua New Guinea and parts of Malaysia, Indonesia and the Philippines - especially in the swampy areas of those countries. There the main species used are Metroxylon and to a much lesser extent Arenga and Caryota.

* The inhabitants of the mangrove-nipa palm zone along the Gulf of Papua in New Guinea subsist almost entirely on a diet of Metroxylon sago and crabs (Ruddle et al 1978).

Seaweeds are widely eaten in developing countries, just as they are in developed ones such as Japan.

* The green sea lettuce Ulva is eaten in salads, as a cooked vegetable, or in soups, in India, southeast Asia and the Pacific coast of South America.

* Another green seaweed, Caulerpa, is eaten in salads and desserts in the Philippines, Malaysia, Indonesia and Sri Lanka.

* Brown seaweeds such as Sargassum and Turbinaria are cooked in coconut milk, smoked or eaten fresh throughout Polynesia as well as in China, the Philippines, Indonesia and Malaysia.

* The red seaweeds, especially Porphyra, Gracilaria, Laurencia and Rhodymenia, are consumed even more widely throughout the Indo-Pacific region (Naylor 1976). Gracilaria is also used in Trinidad and Jamaica to make jellies (Chapman 1970).

Seaweeds also provide valuable gums: agar, algin and carrageenan, derived respectively from red seaweeds such as the Gelidium species, brown seaweeds such as Macrocystis pyrifera and the Laminaria species, and red seaweeds such as Chondrus, Gigartina and Eucheuma (McNeely and Pettitt 1973; Selby and Wynne 1973; Towle 1973).

Among the developing countries, the main producers of red seaweeds are the Philippines, South Korea, Chile, Argentina and China. China and South Korea are also the largest developing country producers of brown seaweeds (FAO 1980b).

Seaweed extracts enter a great many products. Top quality agar is almost uniquely valuable in microbiology as an all-purpose culture medium; and algin is used in paints, dyes, building materials (such as insulation products, sealing compounds, artificial wood), fire-extinguishing foams, paper products, oil drilling lubricants and coolants, cosmetics, shampoos and soaps (Naylor 1976).

Land plants also provide gums, of which gum arabic or gum acacia is the most valuable. The bulk of top quality gum arabic comes from Acacia senegal in Sudan. Lesser quantities, generally of lower quality, come from the same species elsewhere in Africa; and of a still lower quality from another species, A. seyal. Sudanese production is variously reported as coming from cultivated trees (Duke 1981), wild trees (Robbins and Matthews 1974), and both (Adamson and Bell 1974; Glicksman and Sand 1973; Obeid and Seif El Din 1970). Although some plantations or "gum gardens" have been planted by man, most gum comes from wild-sown trees that are more or less managed.

Gum arabic is used in pharmaceuticals, inks, candy and bakery products, for thickening colours and dressing fabrics, and in glues (Duke 1981; Glicksman and Sand 1973). It is widely used in adhesives for postage stamps, small quantities going to "almost every country in the world where stamps are made" (Glicksman and Sand 1973).

Another valuable gum, which currently comes entirely from the wild, is gum karaya, a large bushy tree (Sterculia urens) growing on the dry, rocky hills and plateaus of central and northern India. Its main uses are in pharmaceuticals (as a bulk laxative and as a denture adhesive), paper (as a binder), and foods (as a stabiliser in salad dressings, sherbets, ground meat preparations and meringues) (Goldstein and Alter 1973). Demand for gum karaya is so high that the wild stands have been tapped excessively. Collection is now strictly controlled and trial cultivation has begun (National Academy of Sciences 1979).

Tropical rain forests in the Americas and Asia yield a number of latexes that provide income to local communites. Gutta percha from Palaquium gutta and closely related species, principally in Malaysia and Indonesia, is used in golf balls. Other latexes end up in the higher grades of chewing gum and bubble gum; the lower grades making do with synthetics (Robbins and Matthews 1974; Schery 1972; Whitmore 1973). These latexes are:

* Chicle from the sapote (Manilkara zapota), found wild throughout Central America but largely supplied from Guatemala and Mexico;

* Balata, letchi caspi and sorva gum from Couma rigida and C. macrocarpa, trees of the Amazon basin;

* Jelutong or pontianale from Dyera polyphylla, restricted to peat swamp forests in Borneo.

Chapter 5

FUELWOOD, FIBRES AND AFTERSHAVE

THE MOST WIDESPREAD use of wild plants in developing countries is for fuel and fibre. Trees and shrubs provide energy for cooking and heating in virtually every developing country; and palms, grasses and an array of other wild plants are used for buildings, furniture, and household articles such as mats, baskets and cookingware.

Since the use of wild plants for <u>fuel</u> usually goes unrecorded, estimates vary widely. For example, according to FAO about 90% of the wood consumed in India is for fuel (FAO 1977b); Indian sources tend to place the proportion much lower: around 60%.

One Indian authority, however, calculated that in 1970/71, out of 215 million cubic metres of wood cut, only 12 million cubic metres (6%) was officially recorded (Sharma 1978). Unrecorded sources of fuelwood include community lands, farmlands, waste-land, and wood poached from forest reserves.

Sharma's view is supported by Eckholm (1979), who observes that in the Indian state of Gujarat the official take of wood from forest reserves accounted for only 200,000 tons (4%) of the 4.8 million tons consumed in 1975. The rest came from community lands, from imports, from other states, or was poached.

Probably the most reliable estimates of fuelwood and charcoal consumption in developing countries are those of FAO, which have been discussed by Arnold and Jongma (1978). Except where stated otherwise the following paragraphs are based on their review; all the figures cited in the rest of this section are estimates, although to avoid tedium the qualifier "estimated" has been dropped.

More than 1,200 million cubic metres of wood are used annually by developing countries for fuel. Virtually all of this wood is from wild trees and shrubs, only a negligible proportion currently coming from plantations. This proportion will increase as more plantations become established and as accessible supplies of wild wood grow more scarce.

South and East Asia account for just over half of developing country fuelwood consumption. There, the burning of 693 million cubic metres of wood supplies almost 30% of the total energy used (excluding human and animal energy). As can be seen from Figure 5, the contribution of wood fuels to total energy supply ranges from 6% in West Asia to 66% in Africa.

In East and West Africa the contribution is higher than for
Africa as a whole: 75%; and in some African countries it can be
higher still - for example, almost 95% in Upper Volta, where
fuelwood absorbs 20-30% of annual income (Arid Lands Information
Center 1980).

Not surprisingly there is a similar variation in the importance
of wood fuels within countries as there is among them. Fuelwood
is most important for the urban and rural poor for whom it is the
main energy source for cooking and heating. In the rural areas of
the Bolivian Andes, the Tanzanian plateau, northern Nigeria and

Figure 5. Fuelwood consumption in selected developing regions,
showing contribution of wood fuels to total energy supply
(excluding human and animal energy) (Arnold and Jongma, 1978).

	Fuelwood consumption (million cubic metres)	Contribution to total energy supply (%)
FRICA		
ast Africa	117	75
est Africa	110	75
orth Africa	55	41
otal	282	66
SIA & PACIFIC*		
outheast Asia & Pacific	278	62
outh Asia	267	43
hina and other Asia	148	9
otal	693	29
ATIN AMERICA		
outh America	199	29
entral America	33	9
otal	232	20
EAR EAST		
otal	13	6

excluding Near East

elsewhere, there is no alternative fuel. In Northern Mexico, where incomes are higher, fuelwood supplies less than 30% of energy used. In the state of Bihar, India, where wood is so scarce that dung has to be burned instead, fuelwood accounts for just under 25%.

On average, wood fuels probably contribute 85% of the energy used in rural areas. The proportion drops in zones of relative economic prosperity or ecological adversity.

Fuel is easily the main use for the wood cut in developing countries. About 85% of the annual cut goes up in smoke - mostly for domestic purposes and local agricultural processing. Perhaps half of the fuelwood consumed is for cooking; a third for boiling water, heating houses, and so on; and the rest for agricultural processing and for industries such as brickmaking. In Thailand about 75% of the wood used is for fuel; in Haiti and Bangladesh fuelwood accounts for almost 95% of wood consumption (FAO 1981b).

Almost all Haitians (97%) cook with wood or charcoal, and many thousands of people survive only on the income earned from producing charcoal. Urban consumption of charcoal is rising so rapidly that in some areas deforestation is 25 times faster than reforestation (Library of Congress 1979a).

Firewood and charcoal production have also been increasing in Liberia: from 991,000 cubic metres in 1966 to 1,366,000 cubic metres in 1976 (FAO 1977b). But the proportion of the wood consumed as fuel has been declining steadily since the mid-1960s, when it was 90%, to 67% in the mid-1970s, because of an even faster growth in industrial timber production.

Firewood and charcoal are the principal domestic fuels in Africa and Southeast Asia "for nearly all rural households and about 90% of urban households", say Arnold and Jongma. But fuelwood is also widely used for commercial purposes. Charcoal is burned in commercial food preparation and laundries, and firewood in brickmaking and the manufacture of cement. Tobacco curing in Tanzania in the early 1970s was calculated to require 1.1 million cubic metres of fuelwood for a year (Openshaw 1971). Tobacco curing and rubber preparation in Thailand in the same period absorbed about 300,000 cubic metres a year.

Guatemala provides a fairly representative picture of the importance of fuelwood to developing countries and of the uses to which fuelwood is put. Wild wood is the country's chief energy source. More than 90% of all wood cut is used for fuel, and this is the major cause of deforestation. The chief consumers of firewood are domestic cooking, brick production, lime production, coffee drying and bakeries. About 600,000 rural families use firewood for cooking, accounting for some 1,800,000 felled trees a year.

The limekilns of Cabrican, in Quetzaltenango Dept, account for 60-75 tons of firewood a week, or about 13,000 trees a year. One

About 85% of the wood cut in developing countries is used as fuel - mostly for domestic cooking and heating, or for local agricultural processing.

Brazil: Earthscan photo by Marcos Santilli

The widespread clearance of tropical forests for cattle-ranching, road-building and development is reducing the long-term productivity of the land.

Brazil: Earthscan photo by Marcos Santilli

town (El Tejar) has 82 brick furnaces with a combined firewood consumption of 9,500-10,000 trees a year. The 300 or so coffee estates in Guatemala burn some 40,000 trees a year in the course of coffee drying; and the country's bakeries consume 1,800-2,000 trees a year (Library of Congress 1979b).

Fuelwood demand for agricultural processing and industrial uses is now growing faster than demand for domestic purposes. In Brazil about 4 million tons of charcoal is used in the steel industry and it is planned to increase consumption to reduce reliance on imported coal and coke (FAO 1981a).

How much firewood does a Third World family need? This varies with cooking habits and climate, from about 1.25 million kilocalories per person per year in the warm lowland tropics to more than six million kilocalories per year in cold highlands. This equals from 0.5 cubic metres to more than 2 cubic metres of air-dry fuelwood per person per year.

Average per capita consumption in North Africa is 0.5 cubic metres and in South Asia 0.38 cubic metres. In South America it is 1.03 cubic metres and in East Africa 1.14 cubic metres. The main reason for these differences in per capita consumption (as opposed to per capita requirements) is not climate or cooking habits but physical availability. Migrants from the wood-depleted hills of Nepal to the warmer forested region of the Terai in South Nepal use twice as much fuelwood as the people they left behind.

The heavy demand for fuelwood causes severe deforestation near cities and villages. Arnold and Jongma (1978) cite two towns in the Sahel where the surrounding land is denuded of trees and shrubs, and people must travel 100 kilometres to collect fuel. This accelerates erosion and reduces the productivity of the land, accentuating the misery of the poor, who can no longer afford to buy wood or charcoal, or find journeys to collect firewood getting longer.

There is less time to grow food or earn money. The poverty trap becomes still more difficult to escape, locking the poor into their dependence on the only "free" source of fuel (apart from crop residues and dung): wood from the wild.

Wild plants in the Third World are a major source of materials for construction and for the manufacture of a host of everyday articles. But this obvious fact can be overlooked, and the threat of depletion of some of the more valuable plant groups may come as a surprise.

Despite the ubiquity of galvanised iron roofs, plastics and tin cans, wild plants are still used heavily.

In Bangladesh, for example, wild trees provide telegraph and electricity poles, boxes, matches, pencils, sheds, railway ties, flooring, doors, boats, and are used for house building and the production of paper and mats (Library of Congress 1980a). Such uses of wild plants can be found in every tropical developing country. In this section we will look at just two groups of plants: the bamboos and the palms.

World production of <u>bamboos</u> is currently more than ten million tons a year, mostly in Asia (Sharma 1980). Bamboos are widely cultivated but they are also extensively collected from the wild. Their most important use is in construction, particularly of traditional and semi-traditional houses: bamboos are used for pillars, walls, floors, rafters, and thatching and roofing.

Scaffolding for modern building is often made of bamboo; and India is experimenting with the substitution of bamboo for steel in reinforced concrete. Bamboo is dipped in hot bitumen to repel water and sand-blasted to increase the bond with the concrete. Used in this way bamboo has been found to be a suitable substitute for steel and to reduce production costs by a third (Lessard and Chouinard 1980).

Besides construction, bamboos are used in an astonishing variety of ways. Sharma (1980) lists "sprayers, ropes, tholepins, masts, sails, net floats, basket fish traps, awnings, food baskets, beds, blinds, bottles, bridges, brooms, food, lanterns, umbrella handles, fans, brushes, chains, chopsticks, combs, drogues, dustpans, paper, pens, nails, pillows, tobacco and hookah pipes, anchors, fishing nets, fishing rods, flagpoles, hats, ladles, lamps, musical instruments, mats, tubs, caulking materials, scoops, shoes, stools, tables, tallies, traps, joss sticks, back scratchers... walking sticks, lance staves... loading vessels, trays, water and milk vessels... furniture, agricultural implements, fodder, fuel, floats for timber, trellises, flues, handicrafts, sledges, toys, pipes, cooking utensils, tool handles, polo mallets, stabilizers for haystacks, coffins, cart yokes... ladders, containers, stakes, tiles, seed drills, slats, ornamentals, cordage, wrappers, shuttles..."

The most important industrial use of bamboo is in paper manufacture. In India an estimated two million tons (dry weight) of bamboo a year provides about 600,000 tons of paper pulp (Lessard and Chouinard 1980). Generally, however, bamboo contributes most in rural areas, where it is also a significant element of popular culture. Bamboos are valued not only for their utility but also as a vehicle for artistic expression. In Indonesia split bamboos are woven into walls, mats, containers and fences, often with designs characteristic of the community concerned. Bamboos are made into toys, vases, fans, carvings and many other ornamental artifacts (Lessard and Chouinard 1980).

The 12th century Chinese poet Pon-Son-Tung aptly expressed the combined cultural and economic contribution of bamboo to many peoples when he wrote: "A meal should have meat, but a house must have bamboo. Without meat we become thin; without bamboo we lose serenity and culture itself" (Sharma 1980).

Palms have as wide a range of uses as bamboos. The buriti palm
(Mauritia flexuosa) is known as the tree of life because some
Amerindian tribes in the Amazon basin, Venezuela, Guyana and
Suriname depend on it for all aspects of their livelihood: food
and drink, shelter and clothing (National Academy of Sciences
1975; 1979).

Among other valuable South American palms are the babassu
species, Orbignya martiana and O. oleifera.

* The trunk is a building material and the leaves are used
  for roofing and partitions.

* The leaves and leaf ribs are also made into baskets, mats,
  hats and other articles.

* The smoke from firing the green nuts or the green pulp is
  used as a coagulant in local, small-scale rubber
  production.

* The extremely hard shell of the nuts, once made into
  buttons and other household items, is now made into a
  solid fuel, the manufacture of which yields a number of
  chemical byproducts.

* The oil is also made into a lubricant and fuel, as well as
  soap and margarine (Werkhoven and Ohler 1968).

In southeast Asia the most valuable palms for fibre are the
rattans.

* The stems are used for cords, ropes and even hawsers; they
  are made into baskets and other containers, matting,
  furniture, and much else besides.

* Once their sharp covering of spines is removed, the leaves
  are split and woven, sometimes being made into slatted
  blinds; at other times providing thatch for roofs.

* With the spines left on, the leaves are brought into
  service to prevent thieves from climbing fruit trees and
  bats from roosting in rafters. The rattan's whip-like
  spiny cords have gone into the construction of fish traps,
  the reflexed spines barring the fishes' retreat
  (Dransfield 1979a).

The central contribution of rattans to the everyday economy of
the region has been aptly characterised by the botanist E.J.H.
Corner (1966) as "so invaluable to village life that one can
speak of the rattan civilisation of southeast Asia as one can
speak of the tree-palm civilisation of India and the bamboo
civilisation of Indo-China, China, and Japan."

Rattans are the second most important forest product (after
timber) in southeast Asia (Menon 1980). While there is some

small-scale cultivation of rattan in Sumatra, Sabah, Sarawak and
the Andaman Islands, large-scale plantations are restricted to
Central Kalimantan (Borneo) in Indonesia. These grow only two
species (Calamus caesius and C. trachycoleus), both medium
diameter canes. A substantial proportion of the medium diameter
rattan and all the large diameter rattan entering trade,
therefore, is wild (Dransfield 1979b; Menon 1980).

Trade in raw rattan is worth more than $50 million a year. By the
time it is processed, made into furniture and wickerwork and sold
to the consumer, it is worth about $1.2 billion a year (Shane
1977). The industry is predominately rural and labour intensive,
employing an estimated half a million people in collection and
cultivation processing and cottage-scale manufacturing.

In the Philippines, Sarawak and Peninsular Malaysia most of the
collection is done by aborigines; elsewhere it is done by rural
communities living near remote forest areas (Menon 1980). The
collectors take advantage of the roads made by the logging
industry to extract rattan from areas that otherwise would be
inaccessible. Indonesia dominates the trade in raw rattan,
accounting for 90% in 1975 (Shane 1977).

Aware that they would gain much more by selling the manufactured
articles, several countries have started to impose restrictions
on exports of the raw material. Both the Philippines and Thailand
have banned the export of raw rattan (Menon 1980), and the
Philippines now sells almost all its rattan in the form of
furniture and other articles.

Demand for rattan in the furniture industry of Europe and the USA
is growing. With the clearance of tropical rain forests rattan
habitat is disappearing, and there are fears for its long term
availability (Dransfield 1979b).

Timber (including pulp and paper) is the biggest wild product in
trade. The value of developing country exports of wood products
in 1979 was $6 billion, compared with the value that year of
fisheries exports (the next biggest item) of $5.5 billion (FAO
1981a).

During the five-year period 1974-1978, when the average annual
value of developing country exports of timber products was $4.5
billion (FAO 1980d), 25 developing countries received an average
of $10 million a year or more from the export of "forest
products", mostly wood and mostly from the wild (see Figure 6).
Eight of these countries earned an average of more than $100
million a year, and for seven of them exports of wood products
represented 10% or more of their total export income.

Most developing country wood exports are in the form of roundwood
(47%) or sawnwood and panels (45%), the balance (8%) being pulp
and paper. Almost all of the wood comes from tropical hardwoods
in southeast Asia: 84%. Another 14% comes from Africa, and less
than 1% from Latin America (FAO 1981a). By far the biggest

exporters are Malaysia, Indonesia and the Republic of Korea (South Korea), but Korea itself imports its raw material from Malaysia, Indonesia and the Philippines (Erfurth 1974).

The main genera involved, accounting for more than three-quarters of southeast Asian exports, are the dipterocarps (tall hardwoods) Shorea, Parashorea, Dipterocarpus, Dryobalanops (whose resin is called Sumatra camphor and is used in embalming) and Pentacme, and the non-dipterocarp Gonystylus (FAO 1976). Many more genera, though fewer species, make up the export trade from Africa and Latin America (Erfurth and Rusche 1976a; 1976b).

Tropical timbers are used in furniture, panelling, cabinets, boats, sculpture and carving, decorative veneers, plywood, musical instruments, and many other applications.

Figure 6. Developing countries with forest product exports greater than $10 million per year (FAO 1980d).

	Average annual exports (1974-78) of forest products in thousands of US dollars	Percentage of total exports
Malaysia	908,114	16.9
Indonesia	819,986	9.0
Republic of Korea (S. Korea)	407,393	5.1
Ivory Coast	296,825	17.4
Philippines	268,527	9.5
Brazil	201,296	1.9
Chile	153,541	7.1
Gabon	102,529	9.4
Ghana	81,222	8.9
Cameroon	59,755	10.1
Burma	54,576	25.4
Thailand	45,715	1.5
Honduras	45,674	11.2
Congo	34,658	20.0
Papua New Guinea	27,657	4.4
India	27,402	0.5
Liberia	23,456	5.4
Paraguay	19,863	9.3
Morocco	17,135	1.2
Argentina	14,029	0.3
Central African Republic	14,005	22.2
Hong Kong	11,983	0.1
Kuwait	11,775	0.1
Ecuador	10,869	0.9
Guatemala	10,808	1.3

Trees were once widely used to tan skins and hides, but chromium-based and other mineral tanning materials have ousted most vegetable tannins, which currently account for no more than 30% of total world consumption. The three top vegetable tannins in international trade are the cultivated black wattle (Acacia mearnsii) and two groups of wild trees - quebracho (Schinopsis balansae and S. lorentzii) and myrobalans (Terminalia species, mainly T. chebula) (Robbins and Matthews 1974).

The future of quebracho is somewhat in doubt, since the trees (found in northern Argentina and Paraguay) have to be cut down to extract the tannin and there has been heavy overexploitation (Somigliana 1973).

Myrobalan tannin production is a more easily sustainable industry, because the tannin is extracted from the fruit. The trees occur throughout much of India, which is the centre of production, and also in Burma. Myrobalans have been exported to Europe from India since the early Middle Ages, and local use and the export trade continue (Hathway 1959).

Many other wild plants are used for tanning, and while they are of little account in international commerce they are of considerable importance locally. They include the red mangrove (Rhizophora mangle) and legumes such as Acacia nilotica in East Africa and Caesalpinia spinosa in Andean Bolivia, Peru and northern Chile (Duke 1981).

As well as firewood, building timber and fibres, numerous essential oils and oleoresins are collected in small quantities from wild plants, and bring money into remote developing country communities. Probably those of greatest commercial significance come from the arid lands of North Africa and West Asia, and from the tropical forests of Central and South America.

Cedarwood oil is produced from Cedrus atlantica in Algeria and Morocco (also from the deodar (Cedrus deodara) in the Himalayas and the juniper (Juniperus procera) in East Africa), and is used to perfume men's toiletries (Robbins and Matthews 1974). Oleoresins from the North African/West Asian region going into incense and other perfumes include:

* olibanum (once known as frankincense) from Boswellia species, and opopanax and myrrh from Commiphora species, all small trees that are quite widely distributed in the region, although collection is done principally in Somalia;

* galbanum from several species of Ferula in Turkey and neighbouring West Asian countries (Adamson 1971).

In Latin America:

* Paraguay supplies guaiac wood oil from the tree Bulnesia sarmienti;

* Brazil produces rosewood oil from the rain forest tree Aniba rosaeodora and sassafras oil from Ocotea pretiosa;

* Colombia collects the bulk of the region's production of Tolu balsam from Myroxylon balsamum and Copaiba balsam from Copaifera species, all large trees of the rain forest;

* El Salvador collects Peru balsam from a variety of Myroxylon balsamum;

* Honduras gets American styrax from the sweetgum tree Liquidambar styraciflua, found also in Guatemala, Mexico and southern and eastern USA (Adamson 1971).

Tolu and Peru balsams flavour cough syrups, soft drinks, candies, ice cream and chewing gum. Others are used in perfumes: guaiac wood oil as a blender, copaiba balsam as an adulterant, and rosewood oil in its own right. Sassafras oil enters cosmetics and soaps, as do several of the other oils, but perhaps its most interesting use is as a synergist to increase the effectiveness of pyrethroid insecticides (Adamson 1971; Duke 1981; Robbins and Matthews 1974).

Other wild plants play a role in the horticultural trade. Although this is based largely on cultivation, some exotic ornamentals - especially orchids, cacti, and succulents - are collected from the wild. This can have considerable impact on wild populations since many of the species involved are rare. Wild orchids are an increasing item of trade from southeast Asian rain forest countries, as are cacti from South America and Mexico, and succulents from Madagascar.

For example, in one year (1977) Madagascar exported 15.5 metric tons of seed of Pachypodium species (a group of succulents) to the Federal Republic of Germany (Inskipp and Wells 1979). Trade in wild ornamentals is a minor matter at the national level, but it can be a valuable source of income for rural communities and needs to be more closely regulated if it is to be sustained.

Wild plants are a major, and often the only, source of fuel and fibre, particularly in the rural areas of developing countries. Provided that they are not so heavily exploited that adequate supplies completely disappear, they are likely to remain important for some time. At current and foreseeable levels of poverty, many people will not be able to afford alternative sources.

About one third of the world's human population depends on wood for fuel. Scarcely any of this is planted, although in some countries wastes from rubber, coconut and other plantations make up a significant proportion of the "wood" supply. In areas such as the Andes, the Sahel, the Ganges basin and Java, wood consumption is higher than regeneration: many localities are suffering shortages and others will soon do so.

The plight of the millions of poor people dependent on wood fuel has been dubbed "the other energy crisis" - one more severe and intractable than the oil crisis (Eckholm 1975). Overcoming this crisis requires more efficient use of wood (such as through more efficient stoves) and the establishment of fuelwood plantations.

The poor require and will continue to require plants for fuel and fibre. Wild sources cannot sustain this demand. Cultivated sources are needed to replace them.

Chapter 6

HERBS AND MEDICINAL WILDLIFE

WILDLIFE IS THE traditional source of medicines. With the development of modern synthesised drugs, reliance on the wild has diminished; but in developing countries wild plants (and to a lesser degree wild animals) continue to provide medicines for the treatment of physiological and psychological diseases.

Both indigenous and western medicine are practised in parallel in most developing countries. Although the contribution of wildlife to either system has not been determined, the circumstantial evidence is that it is substantial.

Attitudes to indigenous or <u>traditional medicine</u> range from outright dismissal as mumbojumbo to credulous acceptance of every herbal remedy. Until recently, the governments of almost all developing countries looked down on or ignored their traditional medical practitioners and the plant and animal materials used by them. Western scientific medicine was considered to be the only respectable system, and the only one that could be shown to work.

These attitudes are changing. Although traditional medicine's potential contribution to health care is not fully known, it is now the official policy of many developing country governments to encourage it. The World Health Organization (WHO), UNICEF and the UN Industrial Development Organization (UNIDO) also support indigenous medicine. WHO regards it as a rich cultural and natural resource, and a means of increasing the availability of health services, particularly in rural areas (Ch'en 1977). How did this new respectability come about?

* Large segments of the populations of many developing countries - up to 70-80% - continue to depend on traditional remedies (WHO 1977). This is due partly to poverty - the people cannot afford western medicines - and partly to the greater cultural acceptability of traditional systems, including their ability to minister to psychological needs in ways that foreign systems cannot.

* There is an increasing emphasis on primary health care: basic health care that is not only effective but is also affordable by underequipped and underfinanced countries and by the poorer communities within those countries.

* Many governments have adopted policies of greater self-reliance in essential drugs. Traditional medicines are often cheap, readily accepted by consumers and locally available.

A number of developing countries are trying to integrate western and indigenous medicine. This requires the scientific evaluation of traditional medicines, larger scale manufacture with better quality control, and training in the use of herbal remedies.

* Bangladesh has ten large Ayurvedic factories producing plant medicines;

* Madagascar and Rwanda have taken their traditional pharmacopoeias as the starting point for the research and development of new drugs;

* Thailand has operated a research programme since 1965 to develop modern drugs from native plants (UNIDO 1978).

The rehabilitation of indigenous medicine means a renewed interest in medicinal plants, despite the curiosity evoked by concoctions of rhino horn or pangolin scales. In Africa 95% of traditional drugs are claimed to come from plants (Farnsworth 1977). Of the approximately 2,000 drugs used in the Hindu system of Ayurvedic medicine in India, about 1,500 come from plants, (Singh et al 1979). The twin pillars of Chinese traditional medicine are acupuncture and herbs (C.-C. Chou 1977; Lewis and Elvin-Lewis 1977).

WHO's inventory of medicinal plants lists some 21,000 names for about 10,000 different species (Penso 1978; 1980). What proportion of these is wild, cultivated or both is impossible to say for sure; but on the basis of published accounts of major traditional medical systems, such as the Ayurvedic, the Chinese and the Muslim Unani, it is reasonable to assume that a great many are obtained from the wild.

Most of the several hundred plants still used in India (Gupta 1981), virtually all of the medicinal plants used in Nepal (Singh et al 1979), and most of Sri Lanka's medicinal plants (Pinto 1978) come from the wild. In China, where agricultural ecosystems have replaced natural ones in the plains, medicinal plants are cultivated; but in mountainous parts of the country, where natural vegetation persists, collection from the wild is still the main source of supply (C.-C. Chou 1977).

Animals - generally, it seems, wild animals - are not unimportant in traditional systems. The materia medica of the Lao People's Democratic Republic, for example, includes such animal products as deer antlers; buffalo and rhino horns; tiger, crocodile, bear and pig teeth; monkey and crow bones; and bear and tiger bile. But these remedies are overshadowed by the 2,500 plant types that make up the bulk of the Lao pharmacopoeia (Polsena 1977).

Do indigenous plant drugs work and are they safe? The customers clearly have faith in them; but many developing country health authorities have embarked on the difficult process of evaluation. Traditional remedies are not always amenable to standard scientific analysis, partly because both disease and treatment

Traditional medicines are still widely used in developing countries, with many of the remedies coming from wild plants and herbs; Many developing country governments are actively encouraging its practice.

Bolivia: WHO photo by J. Bland

Although only a few drugs used in Western medicine are now manufactured wholly or partly from wild plants, many drugs originated in the wild. One expert claims that oral contraceptives would never have been developed without diosgenin extracted from Mexican yams.

Iran: WHO photo by D. Deriaz

are often bound up with culture, and it can be hard to separate the physiological and psychological effects of a drug.

Many herbal drugs involve several plant species. For example one of the euphorbias, Elaeophorbia drupifera, is used by traditional practitioners in Ghana to treat guinea worm. By itself this plant is so purgative that it kills; so the herbalist mixes the juice with palm nut oil, which makes it nontoxic (Hanlon 1979).

Many traditional medicines are unquestionably useful. Their study in Ghana has revealed herbs effective for the treatment of post-natal bleeding, diabetes, and infective hepatitis. One species, Cryptolepis sanguinolenta, is used against malaria, to reduce fever and to cure urinary infections. Microbial tests at the University of Science and Technology, Kumasi, show that the plant is a broad spectrum antibiotic, yet none of the compounds isolated from it so far is a known antibiotic (Hanlon 1979).

The objective of research into herbal medicines is not always to identify and synthesise the chemically pure active principles. WHO and national bodies such as the Pharmaceutical Society of Ghana now recommend simply extracts or dosages of the crude plant (Ch'en 1977; Hanlon 1979). Once the safety of a traditional drug has been scientifically confirmed, the aim is to deliver it to the entire national health service quickly and cheaply.

The efficacy of many indigenous remedies should come as no surprise. Some have long been used in western medicine: atropine (belladonna), morphine (opium), quinine (cinchona) and more recently reserpine (rauvolfia) (WHO 1977). Many traditional medical systems are extremely old: records of Chinese use of medicinal plants go back to 400 BC (C.-C. Chou 1977); and herbal remedies are mentioned in the Sanskrit Rigveda, written as long ago as 4500-1600 BC (Singh et al 1979). The Mexican Institute for the Study of Medicinal Plants has rediscovered several plants from the Aztec materia medica which have cardiovascular anti-diabetic and antiparasitic properties (Agarwal 1978).

China's medical policy is to integrate traditional and western medicine, and it continues to evaluate herbal remedies and to spread the availability of the many proven drugs through cultivation, manufacture, and training (H.-C. Chou 1977). A similar policy is pursued in Nepal, which is also convinced that both systems are necessary for a comprehensive health service. Modern medicines are dispensed from 65 health posts, and traditional drugs drawn from more than 60 plant species are dispensed from 82 Ayurvedic centres (UNIDO 1978).

China, Nepal, Ghana and several other countries are putting into practice the moderate position urged by a WHO official: "Western and traditional medicine should not compete with each other because both are valuable national assets. The former is based on the development of science and technology and the latter is based on national cultural values and experience accumulated by the people over a long period of time" (Nakajima 1977).

The contribution of wild plants to <u>western medicine</u> is more modest, though not unimportant. Of the 200 drugs regarded by WHO as essential (WHO 1979), only five come wholly or partly from wild plants:

* atropine, the antidote and antispasmodic, one source of which is Egyptian henbane (Hyoscyamus muticus) obtained largely from the wild in Egypt;

* hydrocortisone, an important anti-inflammatory in dermatology and ophthalmology, derived notably from diosgenin from the wild yams Dioscorea composita and D. floribunda in Mexico and Guatemala;

* the general antidote ipecacuanha, from wild ipecac (Cephaelis ipecacuanha) in Brazil;

* pilocarpine, used as a miotic (to constrict the pupil) in ophthalmology, from wild jaborandi (Pilocarpus), also in Brazil;

* the muscle relaxant tubocurarine, which is both synthesised and obtainable from pareira (Chondrodendron tomentosum), wild in the forests of southern Brazil, Peru, Colombia and Panama (Morton 1977).

Other widely-used drugs derived from wild plants are:

* The antihypertensive reserpine and the antiarrhythmic ajmaline, both from the serpentwood shrub Rauvolfia, common in Africa, the Caribbean, India and Southeast Asia. Both drugs are obtained almost entirely from wild plants, although there is some cultivation of Rauvolfia serpentina in Asia;

* Physostigmine, used as a muscle relaxant and in opthalmology, is obtained from the calabar bean (Physostigma venenosum), native to West Africa from Sierra Leone to Zaire;

* The cardiotonic strophanthin comes from Strophanthus gratus, a wild vine of West Africa's tropical rain forests (Morton 1977).

Hormones are the second largest category of western drugs (the largest is antibiotics) (Farnsworth 1969a). Most are steroids made by partial synthesis from natural substances. Until 1976 the most important source was diosgenin from several species of yam (Dioscorea) growing in Mexico and Guatemala and in the temperate Himalayan regions of China, India and Nepal. One of the Himalayan species, D. floribunda, is cultivated, but the rest are wild. (Coppen 1979; Manning 1969).

In 1963 Mexican diosgenin accounted for 75% of world steroid production. Although Mexican supplies grew rapidly (from 375 tons in 1963 to 600 tons in 1974), the contribution of diosgenin had slipped to 43% by the early 1970s. The price per kilogram in 1974 was $27.68, yielding Mexico more than $16.6 million. But in 1975 Mexico sharply increased the price of the raw material, encouraging consumers of diosgenin derivatives to turn still more actively to alternative steroid sources. By 1976 Mexican diosgenin had been displaced as the premier steroid source by stigmasterol from soybean oil.

Most oral contraceptives - one of the biggest product groups stemming from diosgenin - are now manufactured by total synthesis. India and China, however, with their own supplies of wild yams, still use diosgenin as the starting material for their oral contraceptives and other steroids (Applezweig 1977; Coppen 1979).

The steroid saga illustrates three features of the use of wild plants in modern medicine. First, wild drug plants can have a staggering influence on the course of medicine and can be a real economic boon to the countries that supply them. One expert has gone so far as to claim that had it not been for the discovery of "Mexican diosgenin as the most versatile and available steroid raw material it is probable that we would not have had oral contraception in our time, or even in our century" (Applezweig 1977).

The second feature is the price consciousness of the pharmaceutical industry. If a wild plant's advantages (comparatively low cost, abundance, and security of supply) disappear, the industry will turn to other sources or resort to total synthesis.

The third feature is that synthesis may be unnecessary. Diosgenin-yielding species of Dioscorea occur throughout the tropics, and China and India continue to use diosgenin because adequate supplies of Dioscorea yams are locally available. WHO recognises that a number of essential drugs can be produced from plants that grow wild or are readily cultivated in developing countries - experts at a 1978 UNIDO technical consultation identified more than 100 such biologically active plant species. Of these, 43 are available only from the wild, and an additional 23 are available from both wild and cultivated sources.

The meeting also identified 33 essential drugs and 21 important second category drugs suitable for production by developing countries. Of the former, eight come only from wild plants and another 13 come from plants that are both wild and cultivated. Of the latter, 12 come from wild plants and an additional seven from plants in the wild/cultivated category (UNIDO 1978). The advantages of using locally available wild and cultivated medicinal plants are obvious. Thailand, for example, has 177 modern drug factories, which import more than 90% of their raw materials. It also has more than a thousand traditional drug factories, which obtain 90% of their raw materials from native plants (UNIDO 1978).

Moreover, the export of medicinal plants provides several developing countries with useful revenue. Thailand, for example, earns $1-3 million a year from the export of drug plants, and Nepal gets $1-6 million a year (UNIDO 1978). Commercial cultivation of medicinal plants in Nepal is in its infancy, so at present the country's exports are met entirely from the wild. Most of the trade is with Europe (Belgium, France, United Kingdom), Canada, and East Asia (Hong Kong, Japan, Singapore) (Singh et al 1979).

Wild animals play a much less significant role in western medicine than they do even in indigenous medicine. Only about 6% of US prescriptions contain drugs from animal sources - compared with some 25% containing ingredients from higher plants. Almost all of these are from domesticated animals: thyroid hormone from sheep and hogs; conjugated estrogens from the urine of pregnant mares; insulin, oxytocin and vasopressin from cattle and hogs; and enzymes from hogs (pancreatin, pepsin) and oxen (trypsin, chymotrypsin) (Farnsworth 1969b). Wild animals provide a few non-prescription medicaments, such as halibut liver oil and cod liver oil, but little else of medical significance.

But wild animals make a crucial contribution to <u>biomedical research.</u> The most important group is the primates, which because of their close relationship to human beings are essential for the production and testing of vaccines (particularly the poliomyelitis vaccine), safety testing of drugs, and research into malaria, cardiovascular diseases, cancers, hepatitis and several other diseases.

The most important primates for health purposes include the rhesus monkey (Macaca mulatta), the longtail macaque (Macaca fascicularis), the squirrel monkey (Saimiri sciureus), the chimpanzee (Pan troglodytes), the African green monkey (Cercopithecus aethiops), and the owl monkey (Aotus trivirgatus).

The rhesus monkey is the most widely used, especially for polio and other vaccines. Native to India and neighbouring countries, use of wild rhesus monkeys has dropped sharply since India banned exports in 1977. Captive bred animals now supply much of the demand, the rest being met by wild longtail macaques from Indonesia and the Philippines.

Several species have unique uses:

* The chimpanzee for research into hepatitis B;

* the African green monkey for production of SV40 virus-free poliomyelitis vaccine;

* the Central and South American owl monkey is the only known nonhuman animal suitable for malaria chemotherapy and immunology studies (Interagency Primate Steering Committee 1978).

Collectors and the pet trade are major consumers of live animals from the wild. It has been estimated that in 1975 almost 7 million birds, mostly wild, were exported from the Third World, especially from India, Senegal, China, Indonesia, Thailand and Pakistan. India exports almost 2 million wild birds a year and Senegal close to that figure.

The wild bird trade now involves more than 20% of the world's 9,000 bird species, the most popular being the passerines (perching and song birds) and the psittacines (parrots and their relatives) (Inskipp and Wells 1979). International trade in psittacines is estimated at between 750,000 and 1 million birds a year, Japan and the USA each importing about a third of the total (Roet et al 1981).

The main importers are the USA, Japan, Hong Kong and countries of the European Economic Community. The UK retail trade alone is valued at $3.4 million a year.

Developing countries seem likely to follow two parallel paths: the modernisation of indigenous medicine, and increased participation in the development of western scientific medicine. The first path is necessary because indigenous systems contain many drugs and methods of treatment that are effective, safe, inexpensive, culturally acceptable, and rely on locally available resources.

The second path is a likely consequence of the former. Although western drug companies appear to have lost interest in living resources other than microbes (Tyler 1979), this is probably a passing phase. For a while, the developing countries may continue to be essentially passive recipients of the benefits of western medicine. But in time, the results of Third World research into indigenous plant drugs may be expected to influence the course of western medicine, as has been the case in the past.

In both cases wildlife has a valuable contribution to make. Although cultivation of wild plants will be increasingly necessary, collection from the wild could still be important. And in western medicine some species (such as several of the primates) are indispensable. As biomedical research advances and as knowledge of the properties of wild animals and plants improves, additional species may also be shown to be essential.

The future contributions of wildlife to the two medical systems also depend on the extent to which wildlife is conserved. The experts at the UNIDO technical consultation expressed the issue well: "The developing countries should be careful, when using their medicinal plant resources, not to disturb the ecological balance. They should take steps to conserve and preserve the germplasm available and also their forest wealth. Many of these resources will be needed by the drug industry for many years to come" (UNIDO 1978).

Chapter 7

GENES FOR CROPS AND LIVESTOCK

THE DEVELOPMENT of new domesticated animals and plants, and the improvement of existing domesticates through the transfer of desirable qualities from their wild relatives, are among those uses of wildlife that are almost certain to increase. This value does not tend to decline with industrialisation. In fact, judging from the experience of agriculture, the more intensively managed the crop the more likely it is to draw on the genetic resources available from the wild.

The term "genetic resources" is used here to mean those heritable characteristics of plants and animals that are of actual or potential use to people. The characteristic may be disease resistance, a pharmacological activity, an environmental adaptation, or the capacity of a timber tree to grow tall and straight. As long as it is, or could be, of some economic or cultural value and is transmitted genetically, it qualifies as a genetic resource.

Genetic resources can be grouped into four categories:

* Advanced cultivars (a cultivar is a <u>culti</u>vated <u>vari</u>ety) of plants and modern breeds of animals.

* Landraces or traditional cultivars and breeds.

* Wild relatives of domesticated plants and animals.

* Other wild species of use to people.

Here we are concerned only with the third and fourth categories: wild genetic resources. The wild relatives of domesticated plants and animals are valuable for the improvement of crops and livestock. The thousands of other wild species are a rich store of genetic diversity, which in turn provides the raw material for the selection of new crops or domesticated animals or better forms of those that exist already.

The importance of wild plants and animals as sources of food, fuel, fibre, medicine and income is not difficult to grasp. What is much less appreciated is the contribution of genetic variation within the species concerned. Within medicinal species, for example, genetically controlled variation can be a source of unusually high concentrations of valuable compounds, or of low concentrations of harmful compounds.

* One example is the rosy periwinkle (Catharanthus roseus), from which come the compounds vincristine and vinblastine

used to provide relief in leukaemia. The species is native to the Caribbean but is now cultivated in southeast Asia and coastal Africa. A sample of leaves from wild plants growing in Jamaica gave ten times more biological activity than did those of cultivated plants - suggesting that it would be worthwhile to explore the species' native range more thoroughly (Gupta 1981).

* Valuable variation has been found in different populations of Rauvolfia, the source of reserpine and other medically useful alkaloids. The range of total alkaloids in the African species R. vomitoria from Senegal to Uganda runs from 0.2 to 3.0%. The highest alkaloid content, as well as the largest proportion of reserpine (0.3%), is found in samples from Zaire. Of the two ecotypes of the Asian species R. serpentina, one is high in reserpine but low in total alkaloids, the other is the opposite (Gupta 1981).

* Wild populations of the poppy Papaver bracteatum growing in northern Iran have been discovered to be rich in thebaine (from which codeine and a number of other essential drugs can be synthesised) yet to contain negligible quantities of opium (Fairbairn 1976).

Genetic variation within wild species is the major resource of forestry, pasture improvement and aquaculture, all three of which are in their infancy compared with agriculture and horticulture. Afforestation is still concerned primarily with the development of domesticates from wild species. The main emphasis is not on breeding but on identifying and selecting the most suitable provenance (geographical source of a particular collection of seed or other reproductive material) for planting under local soil and climate conditions (Willan 1973).

Until recently much of this selection was casual and haphazard rather than through examination of the available genetic variation. Sometimes the result was fortunate, as with the introduction into Trinidad of a Burmese provenance of teak Tectona grandis that is fast-growing and of good stem form. At other times it was unfortunate, as with the introduction into Sudan of a provenance of the gum Eucalyptus microtheca with "atrociously crooked stems" (Willan 1973).

Not surprisingly, foresters throughout the world are now much involved in provenance trials. Formal evaluation and selection of the best adapted provenances have already yielded good results.

* Selected provenances of the Central American pines Pinus caribea and P. oocarpa have greatly improved the productivity of plantations in East Africa (A. Greaves pers com), and Mexican provenances of P. pseudostrobus have done well in Malawi (Veblen 1978).

* The best provenances of the Australian gum Eucalyptus camaldulensis were shown to produce three times the volume

of wood than the poorest provenances when tested in
Nigeria (Guldager 1975).

* A Mexican form of the otherwise bushy ipil-ipil (Leucaena
leucocephala) grows into a tall tree. The trees
grow so fast that in the Philippines they regularly
produce 30-50 cubic metres of wood per hectare per year
(by contrast, a well-managed pine plantation under
temperate conditions produces on average about ten
cubic metres/hectare/year), and one stand has even
produced more than 100 cubic metres/hectare/year (National
Academy of Sciences 1979).

The variation within Leucaena leucocephala has also been put to
good use in the development of the plant as a forage crop. Some
wild forms produce much greater quantities of edible forage (feed
for animals) than others, and crosses between such forms can
produce still more (Duke 1981).

Breeding of legumes and grasses for pasture is comparatively
recent. Although the number of bred cultivars is growing, the
majority of tropical varieties currently in cultivation are
collected from natural rangeland or selected from introduced wild
species (Bogdan 1977).

Most aquaculture involves so little "culture" that it scarcely
deserves the name. Essentially it amounts to taking care of wild
aquatic animals during certain periods in their lives to ensure a
higher, more accessible yield than would be obtained if nature
were left to take its course.

In Asia, where aquaculture is of greatest economic importance,
most fish spawn comes from the wild. In Bangladesh only 15% of
the spawn required for aquaculture is produced from cultivated
sources; and India produces less than 10% of its fish spawn
artificially (Davy and Chouinard 1981).

There are few recent Third World examples of the identification
of a new wild species worth domesticating.

* The University of Chile's Institute of Food Technology
learned how to domesticate the wild toad Calyptocephalella
caudiverbera, and has started farms large enough to
produce 50,000 of the animals a year, or 10-15 tons a year
of toad legs. Reported to taste like a cross between
lobster and chicken, the wild toads have long been a
delicacy in Chile. Now that they can be farmed,
researchers and farmers expect ready sales on the
international frogmeat market (Vietmeyer 1981).

* In Nigeria, the Institute of Oil Palm Research is
domesticating the giant African land snail Achatina. The
snails contain as much protein weight for weight as
beef, and more of the important amino acids lysine and
arginine than eggs. Growing rapidly to as much as half a

pound (nearly 250 grams) each, the snails appear to be an ideal source of animal protein. They can easily be reared on small village plots as well as on large plantations (Vietmeyer 1981).

As each economic or useful species develops, genetic variation becomes more and more important. First there is the selection of the strains that perform best. These are hybridised within the crop. Eventually, the crop is "back-crossed" with related wild species to regain features such as disease resistance lost in the process of domestication, or to meet such new demands of the market as mechanised harvesting and long-distance distribution.

Some crops are already far along this road: sugarcane has by now received such large infusions of wild genes that the original crop species, Saccharum officinale, is today a complex hybrid.

The importance of wild genetic resources is sure to increase. This will happen both as demand for food and other necessities (including the need for export income) intensifies and as more species are domesticated. In turn the drive to get the highest production from a shrinking per capita area of productive land will put still greater pressure on plant breeders. They will need to develop varieties that yield more, cope more efficiently with the rigours of the environment, and better meet the demands of the market.

In response to these pressures, breeders can be expected to resort more and more to the rich store of characteristics contained in the wild.

A plant breeder seeking a particular quality will tend to look for it first in other modern cultivars of the crop, then among the landraces, and last among the wild relatives. The further the source is from the advanced variety, the more likely it is to contain genes the breeder does not want.

By and large, breeders will resort to the wild only if the crop is genetically rather uniform, and there is therefore insufficient genetic wealth in the cultivated forms; or if the qualities they seek are much more pronounced in the wild forms. For it is an effort to work with wild species. It can be very difficult to achieve fertile crosses. Moreover, once a cross has been made, getting rid of undesirable characters can involve several years of repeated backcrossing.

Black pepper (Piper nigrum), an important crop in several developing countries (particularly India, Indonesia, Malaysia and Brazil), provides an example of the difficulties. The only known sources of resistance to Phytophthora footrot, the crop's most serious disease are the wild Central and South American species Piper columbrinum, P. guiniensis and P. obliquum. Unfortunately, grafts using these species as rootstocks have deterioriated after only four years (Purseglove et al 1981a; de Waard 1980; de Waard pers com).

The Green Revolution introduced high-yield strains of wheat and other grain crops even to remote areas. This forced many primitive strains into extinction, and has increased the reliance on wild genes.

Colombia: UN photo

Wild rubber (Hevea) trees with higher than average yields have been found in Peru, and are now being tested to increase yields in cultivated rubber.

Thailand: FAO photo by S. Bunnag

It is a measure of the value of wild species that, despite the difficulties of working with them, they are already indispensable for the improvement of several crops, and they are being used in the breeding of a great many more. Plant breeders are returning to the wild for a wide range of desirable agronomic features, as the examples that follow show.

The many ways in which wild species have contributed to crop improvement have been reviewed extensively by Harlan (1976), Prescott-Allen and Prescott-Allen (1981) and Stalker (1980). None of these reviews attempts to distinguish between experimental crosses and crosses that have been released to growers, or to evaluate precisely the impact on current production. With the aim of doing this we have been conducting a survey of breeders and other specialists as well as of the literature. The survey is still in progress and the results have not yet been analysed. In the following paragraphs, however, we draw on some of the data collected (cited as PA DATA Crop Survey).

The use of wild species in sugarcane breeding (mainly Saccharum spontaneum) has helped almost to double the cane yield and more than double the yield of sugar (Simmonds 1979).

* Cocoa (Theobroma cacao) yields have been boosted through the incorporation of wild and semiwild material from the upper Amazon into cultivars in West Africa, South America and Southeast Asia. In many cocoa producing countries these cultivars are the only officially recognised planting material. The wild germplasm supplies high yield potential, ease of establishment, precocity, and resistance to several diseases and tolerance of others (see below) (Chalmers 1972; Soria 1975; Toxopeus 1969; PA DATA Crop Survey).

* Yield increases in rubber are being sought from wild material (Majid and Hendranata 1975); wild rubber (Hevea) populations with higher than average yields have been found in the Madre de Dios area of Peru, and the best clones are being tested (Imle 1978).

* A high yield variety of sesame has been developed in India from a cross between southern Indian landraces and the wild gingelly of Malabar (Sesamum indicum var malabaricum) (PA DATA Crop Survey).

Genes from the wild have also brought improvements in quality.

* Wild relatives of cassava, principally Manihot tristis saxicola (found in Suriname and Brazil), have raised the protein content (Hahn et al 1973; PA DATA Crop Survey).

* Gossypium thurberi, which grows wild in Mexico and the USA, has increased the fibre strength of several cotton cultivars (Phillips 1976).

* Greater saturation of oil can be transferred to the African oil palm from the wild Central and South American oil palm Elaeis oleifera (Harlan 1976).

* The tomato has been transformed by its wild relatives. Lycopersicon esculentum cerasiforme and L. hirsutum from Ecuador and Peru, L. peruvianum from Peru and Chile, and the endemic Peruvian species L. pimpinellifolium and L. chmielewskii, have together intensified the cultivated tomato's colour, increased its soluble solids content, and given it more vitamin C (Rick 1977, 1979; Rick and Smith 1953).

Wild species are being used to increase the tolerance of several crops to otherwise unfavourable growing conditions.

* Manihot glaziovii from Brazil has contributed genes for drought resistance in cassava (Jennings 1976).

* In several parts of the world, the range of the wine and table grape has been expanded through crossing with local wild grape species, such as Vitis caribea in the Caribbean Islands and Venezuela (Olmo 1976).

* A number of wild tomato species have great potential for extending the range of the crop: some ecotypes of the tomato Lycopersicon esculentum cerasiforme are tolerant of intense tropical moisture and temperatures, and thus provide source material for the adaptation of the tomato to the wet tropics (Rick 1973; 1976). There are also ecotypes of L. chilense from Chile and Peru and of Solanum pennellii from Peru that are highly tolerant of drought (Rick 1973; 1979); while some ecotypes of L. cheesmanii, endemic to the Galapagos Islands of Ecuador, are tolerant of very high salinities (Rush and Epstein 1976).

* Solanum acaule from Peru, Bolivia and northwest Argentina is widely used in potato breeding programmes for frost resistance, since it generally shows no damage at -8 degrees centigrade or even -10 degrees centigrade (Hawkes 1958).

Other actual and potential contributions by wild species to crop improvement are new modes of reproduction, new cytoplasms, easier crossability, and greater vigour (Prescott-Allen and Prescott-Allen 1981).

* Wild Saccharum spontaneum from Indonesia and India and wild S. robustum from Papua New Guinea have increased the vigour of sugarcane.

* Wild Solanum demissum from Mexico and Guatemala have given new vigour to the potato.

* Wild forms of Theobroma cacao from Peru have done the same for cocoa (PA DATA Crop Survey).

* Pineapple breeders have sought greater vigour, particularly a stronger root system and longer plant life, through crossing the main cultivar "Cayenne" with two wild species - Ananas bracteatus found in Argentina, Brazil, Paraguay and Bolivia and Pseudananas sagenarius found in these four countries and Ecuador (Collins 1960).

* The Rubber Research Institute of Malaysia is using both Hevea pauciflora (wild in Peru, Colombia, Venezuela, Guyana and Brazil) and H. benthamiana (wild in Peru, Colombia, Venezuela and Brazil) as sources of vigour (Imle 1978).

Resistance to pests and diseases is the character most sought from wild species and is the greatest contribution that wild species have made to currently grown cultivars. The following is a representative sample of crops that substantially benefit already, or are likely to soon, from resistance conferred by the wild species of developing countries (unless cited otherwise all data are from PA DATA Crop Survey).

* Minamiyutaka, a Japanese cultivar of the sweet potato, gets its resistance to root-lesion nematode from wild Ipomoea trifida from Mexico (Sakamoto 1976).

* Three varieties of rubber released in Malaysia have some resistance to South American leaf blight obtained from wild Hevea brasiliensis and H. benthamiana from Brazil.

* The resistance of several cassava cultivars to cassava mosaic, cassava bacterial blight and other diseases is derived from Manihot glaziovii and M. dichotoma from Brazil and M. tristis saxicola from Suriname and Brazil.

* Wild forms of avocado (Persea americana) from Mexico, Central America and northern South America provide rootstocks resistant to root rot.

* Virtually all cultivars of cotton grown in Sudan are resistant to bacterial blight; the resistance was transferred from the African wild cotton (Gossypium anomalum).

* In Colombia wild forms of Coffea arabica (from Ethiopia) and of C. canephora and C. liberica (both from West Africa) are being used to confer resistance to rust and anthracnose on coffee plants.

* In Argentina wild forms of Capsicum annuum from Mexico have given sweet peppers resistance to Phytophthora footrot.

* Almost all tomato cultivars now have resistance to Fusarium wilt from Lycopersicon pimpinellifolium (from Peru) and to tobacco mosaic from L. peruvianum (from Peru and Chile). Resistance to 12 other diseases of tomato have been transferred from wild species.

* Many tobacco cultivars get their resistance to mosaic from wild Nicotiana glutinosa (from Ecuador and Peru), and to wildfire and black shank from wild N. longiflora and N. plumbaginifolia (both occurring in Argentina, Bolivia, Brazil and Paraguay).

* Solanum demissum (wild in Mexico and Guatemala) occurs in the ancestries of the majority of potato cultivars grown today, contributing some field resistance to blight and in some cases perhaps also to potato leaf-roll virus. Other wild potato species used for disease resistance include S. acaule (from Argentina, Bolivia and Peru) for resistance to virus X and wart races, S. stoloniferum (from Mexico) for resistance to viruses A and Y, and S. vernei (from Argentina) for resistance to nematodes.

* Wild and semiwild Theobroma cacao from the Peruvian Amazon has provided many cocoa cultivars with resistance to witches' broom, swollen shoot, and other diseases.

Sugarcane, maize and rice provide examples of the actual and potential benefits of wild species to crops in the grass family.

* All sugarcanes bred in India are derived from crosses between cultivated Saccharum officinarum and wild S. spontaneum from Indonesia and southern India. India's sugar industry could not have been established without the acquisition of resistance to red rot from Javan S. spontaneum. This same source of germplasm has had a radical influence on the sugarcane crops of other countries, including the USA.

* The biggest contribution to maize improvement that the newly discovered wild perennial corn Zea diploperennis (endemic to Mexico) is likely to make is disease resistance. It is immune to chlorotic mottle virus (a serious disease in South America), and to streak virus (Africa's most serious disease of corn). No other source of resistance to these diseases is known. It also appears to be immune to three other diseases prevalent in the American tropics.

A single sample of wild rice (Oryza nivara) from central India is the only known source of resistance to grassy stunt virus. This virus was once a serious disease of rice in Asia: during the early 1970s epidemics in India, Sri Lanka, Indonesia, Vietnam and the Philippines totally destroyed more than 116,000 hectares of rice. With the release and widespread use of cultivars resistant to grassy stunt virus, the disease has ceased to exist in

IR36 was the first rice cultivar with resistance to all four major Asian
rice pests and all four major Asian rice diseases. Much of this resistance
came from a single sample of wild rice (Oryza nivara) from central India.

South Korea: UN photo

farmers' fields. The first of these, IR28, IR29 and IR30, were released in 1974; but the big breakthrough came in 1976 with the release of IR36, a cultivar bred (like the previous ones) by the International Rice Research Institute in the Philippines.

IR36 was the first cultivar with resistance to all four major Asian rice pests and all four major Asian rice diseases. It derived its resistance to the pests (brown plant hopper, green leaf hopper, stem borer, and gall midge) and to two of the diseases (bacterial blight and tungro virus) from Indian landraces, and to the other two diseases (grassy stunt virus and blast) from Oryza nivara.

Today IR36 is the most widely grown variety of rice in the world, grown on some ten million hectares (25 million acres). Another 20 recommended cultivars of rice with O. nivara in their ancestry are grown on an additional ten million hectares (25 million acres) in India, Nepal, Bangladesh, China, and the countries of Southeast Asia (Khush 1978; 1979; Khush et al 1977; PA DATA Crop Survey). Since the release of these varieties no other source of resistance to grassy stunt virus has been discovered, despite extensive screening, although one cross between rice and another wild species, O. rufipogon, shows sufficient promise to be a candidate for tests.

While the impact of wild plants on plant breeding has been considerable, wild animals have been used scarcely at all in livestock breeding. We have come across only two examples from developing countries.

* In Israel the Sinai desert goat has been crossed with the wild ibex: the resulting hybrid, called the ya-ez (combining the Hebrew words for the two animals), joins the former's hardiness and ability to go for days without water with the tastiness of the latter's meat (Vietmeyer 1981).

* In India two wild tasar silk moths, Antheraea roylei from India and A. pernyi from China, have been hybridised to produce A. proylei. Tasar silk culture, known as wild or forest sericulture because generally the silkworms are left to feed on wild trees and some are themselves wild, is practised in China and India. World production is estimated to be 4,000 tons of silk a year, with India producing 10%. India's output of wild silk provides export earnings of almost $4.5 million a year and gives income and full or part-time employment to more than a hundred thousand tribal families. Silk from A. proylei is claimed to be the finest ever produced in India and the hybrid also outyields its parents by almost 170% in weight of silk and by 94% in filament length. It is a valuable component of plans to expand the tasar silk industry and increase its capacity to provide rural communities with jobs and money (Jolly 1980; Jolly et al 1976).

The richness and potential of wildlife as a resource for the development of new crops and livestock is evident. At present the biggest contributions are being made to forestry and pasture productiion, and aquaculture too is beginning to benefit.

It may be tempting to conclude that all three activities will one day be able to dispense with wild genetic resources. This is most unlikely.

The lesson of breeding in crops and livestock is that domestication inevitably involves a narrowing of the genetic base. Among the genetic determinants that are soon lost are those controlling disease resistance and adaptation to marginal environments. The much improved timber and forage cultivars and aquaculture stocks that can be obtained from further selections from the wild, and from the subsequent cycles of breeding among those selections and the cultivars derived from them, can be expected eventually to need new genetic infusions from the wild to maintain and increase their productivity.

This is what is happening in crop breeding. Yet although wild species are playing a vital role in the improvement of many crops, their potential is still far from being fully explored. There are three reasons for this.

* First, in some crops (such as the Phaseolus beans and pulses) sufficient variation remains within the crop itself to make use of the crop's wild relatives unnecessary for the time being.

* Second, the real difficulties of using many of the wild species can discourage breeders from turning to them except as a last resort.

* Third, even when wild species are clearly the best source of a desired characteristic and are taken into a breeding programme, it can take a long time before an acceptable cultivar reaches the grower. The banana provides an extreme example. The Cavendish clones, which are the basis of the banana export industry, are extremely susceptible to disease. Disease resistance has been found in wild bananas, and these have been used in a programme of crossing and selection that has yielded hybrids that, with further work, promise to combine the desired disease resistance and agronomic excellence. This has taken 15 years. It is estimated that it will take another ten years before the new hybrids can be released (Rowe and Richardson 1975; P.R. Rowe pers com).

But for a number of crops the picture is quite clear. It is likely that tomato and potato breeders, for example, will continue to turn to the wild relatives of their crop species, since most of the variation is there rather than in the cultivars. Increasing emphasis on wild sources of germplasm is also likely in those crops in which, even though they are quite diverse, the particular qualities required by the breeder are missing. The main source of pest and disease resistance in peanuts, for example, is now the wild species (Moss 1980).

Changes in technology and in social expectations are other encouragements to use the greater diversity available in wild species. Cotton breeders are turning to wild cotton species both for better fibre, now that they have the technology to evaluate lint quality precisely, and for pest and disease resistance, now that higher environmental standards and more sophisticated awareness of economic and ecological costs discourage reliance on pesticides (Phillips 1976).

Agriculture originated from wildlife. Today wildlife provides much of the material for its repair and renewal. The future will no doubt bring changes in the ways we use wild genetic resources, but our dependence on them seems unlikely to diminish.

Chapter 8

ECOLOGICAL SUPPORT: FLOODS AND PEST CONTROL

IT IS ALMOST tautological to say that wildlife provides the ecological support for economic activity. Apart from people and their domesticates, the biosphere is wild. Without the biosphere, human survival, let alone economic activity, is not possible.

Ecological support means the provision of essential ecological processes - in the words of the World Conservation Strategy: "those processes that are governed, supported or strongly moderated by ecosystems and are essential for food production, health and other aspects of human survival and sustainable development" (IUCN 1980). They include:

* the cycling of carbon and other vital elements;

* the concentration, fixing and recycling of nutrients;

* the regulation of the chemistry of the planet so that the Earth remains fit for life;

* soil formation, regeneration and protection;

* the cleansing of the air and waters, and waste disposal.

Some processes are so basic to our survival - those regulating planetary chemistry in particular - that paradoxically they appear remote and of little practical interest. Probably this is due to their grand scale, our weak and fragmentary knowledge of them, and the conseqential limitations on our ability to influence them (other than involuntarily). However, there are a number of other levels of ecological support, several of which benefit the everyday lives of a great many people in developing countries in readily understandable ways, and in whose disruption can cause economic and social harm. In this section we look at three such kinds of ecological support - all provided by wild plants and animals in natural and semi-natural ecosystems. They are environmental buffering, nutrient supply and recycling, and ecological services.

In the coastal zone, coral and mangrove ecosystems provide people and property with a buffer against storms and the sea. Unfortunately their value as environmental buffers is seldom appreciated until they have been so damaged that disaster strikes. Not uncommonly these disasters are called natural, even though humans have been instrumental.

In Sri Lanka repeated removal of coral reefs for the production of lime has resulted in the collapse of a fishery; the reduction of mangroves because of soil erosion; the disappearance of small lagoons important as nursery areas for fish; erosion of cultivated coconut land; salinisation of local wells; and salinisation of the soil within half a mile of the shore, which in turn has caused the loss of useful vegetation (Salm 1981).

In India, too, destruction of reefs for lime has exposed coastal areas to erosion by the sea (Government of India 1980). In both India and Bangladesh overexploitation of mangrove areas for fuelwood and timber has resulted in the degradation of an important barrier against cyclones and tidal waves (Government of India 1980; Library of Congress 1980a).

Forests are the prime example of natural areas that contribute to human welfare by acting as environmental buffers. Forests influence local climates, generally by making them milder. They help to provide a continuous flow of clean water; some forests, notably tropical cloud forests, even increase the availablity of water by intercepting water from clouds.

Watershed forests are particularly important because they hold together soil cover and protect areas downstream from floods. Without the sponge-like effect of their vegetation, which retains moisture and releases it slowly, the flow of water becomes erratic, leading to both floods and water shortages. The removal or degradation of watershed forests causes an increased rate of water runoff, which strips away the soil; deprives agriculture of nutrients; raises river beds with debris (so causing more and bigger floods); clogs reservoirs, irrigation systems, canals and docks with silt; and smothers coral reefs (IUCN 1980).

Despite their crucial (if indirect) economic importance, watershed forests are being widely devastated by clearance for agriculture, logging, cutting for fuel, overgrazing, and badly managed road-building.

* In the Philippines an estimated 5 million hectares (12 million acres) of forest lands have been cleared, of which 1.4 million hectares (3.5 million acres) were in critical watershed areas (Library of Congress 1980c). Deforestation in northern Luzon has silted up the reservoir of the Ambuklao Dam so fast that its useful life has been reduced from 60 to 32 years (USAID 1979). By 1985 the reduced lifetime of the reservoir is expected to have cost an estimated $25 million (Library of Congress 1980c).

* In the early 1970s it cost $10 million a year to dredge silt from the estuary of Argentina's River Plate and keep Buenos Aires open to shipping. Yet 80% of the 100 million tons of sediment that every year threatened to block the harbour came from only 4% of the drainage basin: the small but heavily overgrazed catchment area of the Bermejo River 1,100 miles upstream (Pereira 1973).

Despite their critical importance as ecological buffers, watershed forests are being widely devastated by clearance for agriculture, logging, cutting for fuel, overgrazing, and badly managed road-building.

Brazil: Earthscan photo by Marcos Santilli

Coral, mangrove and wetland communities trap and accumulate nutrients from the land, thereby supporting local fisheries. Many island nations depend on the local fishing industry for a significant proportion of their animal protein and of their exports.

Dominica: Earthscan photo by Philip Wolmuth

Indian government reports are full of alarm at the state of the nation's catchment areas. The Sixth Five Year Plan notes that "large scale deforestation in recent decades has rendered the sensitive catchment areas in the Himalaya and other hilly areas particularly vulnerable to soil erosion" (Government of India 1980). An average of six billion tons of soil are lost to erosion each year, taking with them more than five million tons of nitrogen, phosphorus and potash with an annual replacement of well over $1 billion.

Of the 75 million hectares (185 million acres) classified as forest land, less than half is under adequate tree cover, and as much as 20 million hectares (50 million acres) is affected by erosion (Government of India 1980). One report puts the situation in even starker terms: "95 million hectares (235 million acres) represent more or less denuded land surfaces whose contribution to the national economy is disastrously negative in character. For not only do these lands not produce trees or grasses to anything like their potential, but they are today the main source of soil erosion and of all the evils that this leads to." (Vohra 1978).

Much of the silt and debris released by this accelerated erosion is washed to sea. The remainder clogs water supply and hydroelectric reservoirs, irrigation channels, harbours and waterways. Loss of storage capacity is a major and expensive problem. The capacity of the Nizamsagar Reservoir has been more than halved, from almost 900 million cubic metres to fewer than 340 million cubic metres. Now there is not enough water to irrigate the 110,000 hectares (270 million acres) of sugarcane and rice for which it was intended, and hence not enough sugarcane to supply local sugar factories (Das 1977).

India's investment in reservoirs is of the order of $12 billion (Government of India 1980), but major reservoirs are silting up at rates several times faster than those projected at the time of their construction (Vohra 1978). "In most cases", says the Sixth Five Year Plan, "alternative sites for storage dams are just not available even if we can find the large sums of money needed to build new reservoirs in place of those which go out of commission" (Government of India 1980).

Every year floods caused by India's silted river beds on average do more than $1 billion of damage to crops, livestock, buildings and communications, as well as causing enormous distress and suffering. The total area subject to periodic floods has doubled in a mere ten years, from 20 million hectares in 1971 to 40 million hectares (50-100 million acres) today (Government of India 1980). Deforestation in Nepal and Himalayan India is heavily implicated in the increase in magnitude and severity of India's floods.

The Himalaya is a young and geologically unstable system, and high rates of erosion are natural, but half current erosion is attributed to the loss of forests. This in turn has at least doubled the sediment load of rivers and sometimes quadrupled it. Consequently the beds of rivers flowing across Nepal's Terai plain have been rising by 15-30 cm (6-12 inches) a year. One of these rivers, the Kosi, whose floodwaters surge across the Terai with no defined banks for four months of the year, has been dubbed "Bihar's Sorrow" because of the floods it causes in the Indian state of Bihar (Library of Congress 1979c; 1980b).

Destruction of watershed forests leads to water shortages as well as floods. Water that would otherwise have been retained in the subsoil or recharged groundwater aquifers instead runs off immediately. The water that would normally have supplemented river flow during the dry season is thus no longer available, with the result that areas subject to floods can also fall victim to drought (Government of India 1980).

Human beings have long depended on natural systems to supply them with nutrients. A great many people in developing countries still depend on tropical forests to restore fertility to the soils that they farm. More than 200 million people occupying about 12 million square miles (31 million sq km)of tropical forests live by shifting agriculture, meaning that they farm an area for a few years, then clear another area, leaving the first one fallow to revert to scrub and forest. The fallow period generally lasts from eight to 12 years in tropical rain forests and from 20 to 30 years in drier areas. During this time the re-established forest cover enables the soil to regenerate.

This is stable productive practice if the human population itself is stable. But if populations are growing, which nowadays they usually are, the pressure on land increases, fallow periods shorten, the forest has no chance to recover, the soil does not regenerate, and larger and larger areas of otherwise productive tropical forest are destroyed (FAO 1978c; IUCN 1980).

Tropical forests concentrate scarce nutrients until there are enough to make cultivation feasible, albeit for only a few years. Natural rangelands perform the equivalent function for livestock rearing. Rangelands are marginal for agriculture largely because they are poor in water, but sometimes also because their soil is poor. They can be very productive, however, converting the available nutrients into grasses, which livestock can then reconvert into the economically more liquid forms of meat, hides and wool.

Bolivia's Altiplano is a good example. Covering 172,000 square kilometres (66,400 sq miles) of the high Andes, the Altiplano is generally dismissed as cold and infertile. Yet it is "potentially one of the richest, most productive grasslands in the world, rivalling or exceeding the best natural range in the United States" (Freeman et al 1980). One site that has been protected from overgrazing was found to produce 6,660 kilograms of forage per hectare (5,900 lb/acre), greater than any range in the US. Moreover, as overgrazed range was allowed to recover, unpalatable species were replaced by palatable ones (Freeman et al 1980).

Thus the Altiplano's natural communities of grasses make nutrients available to people that otherwise would be lost to them or extremely difficult for them to use sustainably.

This valuable phenomenon seems to have been well appreciated by the Incas (12-16th century AD), for whom grazing was the main production system. The constraints of soil and climate limited agriculture, and the grasslands were well suited for llama and alpaca as they are today.

As Freeman and his colleagues (1980) describe it: "The Indians of the Altiplano seemed to the Europeans to be extraordinarily wealthy. The 'secret' to this wealth was thought by the Europeans to be the hundreds of thousands of alpacas and llamas grazing on the Altiplano. This mistake of thinking animals, not grass, are the 'secret' to wealth, was not made by the Incas."

The wildlife of marine and coastal ecosystems also makes significant contributions to developing country economies by making available and recycling nutrients. Without their activity the nutrients would be far too dispersed for people to be able to use them.

Fish, for example, are obliging enough to move in shoals; if they were distributed uniformly about the oceans, their frequency would be so low that it would be too expensive to catch them.

Coral communities scavenge and concentrate ocean nutrients, and mangrove and other wetland communities trap and accumulate nutrients from the land. This allows the consumption and redistribution of the nutrients by fish, crustaceans and molluscs, and in turn by the people who catch and eat them.

In tropical estuaries, lagoons and other shallow waters, marine plants often contribute a major portion of total photosynthetic production. For example, the 175 square kilometre (68 sq mile) seagrass meadow in Tarut Bay, Saudi Arabia, has been calculated conservatively to produce a minimum of 228,000 tons (wet weight) of fresh growth a year. The energy equivalent of this production is 140 billion kcal per year - the equivalent of 95,000 barrels of oil. A significant proportion of this energy is converted to useful products such as shrimp, fishes, and sea turtles; but besides converting solar energy into forms that are directly beneficial to people, the seagrass meadow also provides nursery areas and other critical habitats (see below) for a variety of marine animals (Basson et al 1977).

Ecological services here mean specific services performed by wildlife to the benefit of agriculture, forestry, fishing or any other economic activity based on living resources.

The service may be provided by a particular species (such as pollination of crops by wild insects, birds or bats), or by the contributions of naturally occurring predators and parasites to programmes of biological and integrated pest control. Or they may

be provided by communities of wild species, notably the provision
of critical habitat for species of direct economic or cultural
value.

Many crops are insect-pollinated, but in most cases domesticated
bees are used. This may be because the crop is an exotic and
therefore lacking in native pollinators; or because the crop may
be grown so extensively that there are insufficient wild
pollinators available; or because the domesticated bees are more
efficient and reliable. Nevertheless some crops are pollinated
largely or exclusively by wild insects.

* Cocoa is pollinated by midges belonging to the Ceratopo-
  gonidae.

* The main pollinators of mango are probably wild flies (for
  example, Syrphus, Musca, Psychonosma) and wild bees.

* In Mexico and Central America squashes are pollinated by
  the squash bees Peponapis and Xenoglossa. These wild bees
  get their pollen exclusively from wild and domesticated
  cucurbits, of which they are highly efficient pollinators.
  However, they do not occur outside the Americas, and
  elsewhere squashes are pollinated by domesticated bees or
  by hand (Free 1970).

* Vanilla, which is native to Central America and Mexico,
  must be pollinated by hand outside its native region. In
  its home ground vanilla is pollinated by wild bees of
  the genus Melapona, although in Mexico supplementary
  pollination by hand is also carried out (Purseglove et al
  1981b).

Well-documented examples of natural control of pests are rare.
One comes from Indonesia where the main predators of the corn
borer moth are wolf spiders of the genus Lycosa. Experiments by
the International Rice Research Institute have shown that
traditional Javanese systems of intercropping peanuts and maize
reduce corn borer infestation by encouraging predation by the
spiders. The wolf spiders were slightly more effective at
reducing infestation than the selective biological insecticide
Bacillus thuringiensis, and almost three times more effective
than regular applications of the broad spectrum insecticide
Azinophosmethyl (IRRI Cropping Systems Program 1973).

Critical habitats include feeding, breeding, nursery and resting
areas that are crucial for the survival of a given species. The
critical habitat for one wild species is often provided by
aggregations or communities of other wild species. In this way
all of the wild plants and animals mentioned in this report
depend for their survival on a great many other wild organisms.

The wild plant communities of the coastal zone provide critical
habitat for many important fish and crustacean species and so
help to maintain developing country fisheries. Many valuable

shrimp species breed at sea, after which the young move into mangroves or seagrass meadows where they seek both food and shelter.

In the Indian Ocean several species of shrimp (Penaeus semisulcatus and P. latisulcatus, for example) depend on seagrass meadows for shelter during their juvenile stages. Others (including P. indicus, P. merguiensis, P. monodon and most Metapenaeus species) rely on mangroves for nursery areas, although Metapenaeus will remain in the lagoons after the trees have been removed.

Mangroves also provide nurseries for such commerically important fishes as mullets (Mugil), grunts (Pomadasys) and milkfish (Chanos) (MacNae 1974). Figure 7 shows the correlation between mangroves and shrimp fisheries in areas of the Indo-Pacific for which complete data have been gathered.

Figure 7. Correlation between certain mangrove areas and shrimp fisheries (MacNae 1974).

	Sq km of mangroves	tons/year of shrimp taken offshore
Mozambique	858	2309
Madagascar	3207	4300
W.Thailand	1500	3300
Malaya	3000	ca. 32000
Irian Jaya, Papua New Guinea and N. Australia	4400	ca. 10000

All human activities depend ultimately on ecological processes, including some which do not involve wildlife as defined in this report, which excludes microorganisms. Thus the fertility of permanent agricultural land relies heavily on microorganisms such as the rhizobial bacteria associated with legumes. And phytoplankton are the most important primary producers in the majority of the world's oceans and form the base of the food web for most temperate region fisheries (Basson et al 1977).

Wild microorganisms play a major and often the dominant role in a number of ecological processes of great importance for developing countries. The environmental buffering provided by watershed forests, coral reefs and mangroves is a benefit to all people who live and work in river basins and the coastal zone. Since 40% of the world's population live in the plains adjacent to mountainous areas (FAO 1978d) and a great many live along coasts, this is a considerable contribution.

The other kinds of ecological support - nutrient supply and recycling, and ecological services - are more specific to particular activities. These activities directly support hundreds of millions of people in developing countries.

These various forms of ecological support are free goods (apart from the opportunity costs involved in not destroying the ecosystems that govern them). Although not entered as benefits in national accounts, when they are removed or reduced by bad planning or misuse their absence is clearly felt as a cost.

Chapter 9

DEVELOPMENT NEEDS CONSERVATION

IT IS CLEAR from the previous chapters that wildlife makes a major contribution to the lives and economies of people in developing countries. Much animal protein comes from the wild, and in certain areas wild plants probably supply a significant proportion of essential vitamins and trace elements. Wild plants and animals are also valuable sources of dietary variety.

Most fuel for cooking and heating comes from wild trees and shrubs. For a great many communities, particularly rural ones, inflation and rising oil prices have ruled out alternative fuels even though firewood is seriously depleted. Wild plants continue to be a readily available, low cost source of raw material for housing and for household articles such as mats, containers and furniture.

Wild plants also play a central role in traditional medicine, a role likely to persist with the modernisation of indigenous medical systems and their integration with western medicine. Western medicine itself benefits from wildlife, since some drugs are still obtained from wild plants, and wild animals are important for biomedical testing and research.

Forestry and fishery products are likely to be significant generators of export income for as long as they are available, even though for many countries they contribute only a modest percentage of total income. Regardless of the size of wildlife's contribution to national economies, its contribution to local economies is - and may well continue to be - crucial. Wild plant and animal products constitute one of the few means by which many rural communities can earn money. And they provide one of the few ways in which rural communities can hope to build a modest industrial base.

Wildlife also makes an important contribution indirectly, by providing genetic resources and ecological support. The abundance of useful properties available in the wild are developing new and better crops. At the same time, several existing crops have been improved with genes from wild plants, and the prospects are that plant breeders will continue to draw increasingly on wild genetic resources for disease resistance and other valuable qualities.

Wildlife and wild ecosystems protect watersheds and coasts, providing a buffer against harmful environmental perturbations such as floods and drought. In addition, they recycle and increase the availability of nutrients, and provide several valuable ecological services, notably critical habitat for economically, genetically and ecologically important wild species.

Besides its utilitarian importance, wildlife plays a major part in the cultures of developing countries. This type of contribution to the quality of life is often overlooked, perhaps because it is assumed - incorrectly - that poor people are concerned only with material things.

Although the subject is outside the scope of this report, it is worth noting that the nonutilitarian values of wild plants and animals can be of very great importance. Indeed it is hard to separate the economic from the social and cultural aspects of wildlife. For people in developing countries, as in developed countries, food is valued for taste, texture, prestige, symbolism and a variety of other features that have little if anything to do with nutrition. Similarly, the physiological efficacy of traditional cures may frequently be indistinguishable from their psychological effects.

Wildlife is also valued in developing countries for its own sake, just as it is in developed countries. For example, the baobab tree (Adansonia digitata) is protected by many peoples in Africa's savanna zone. Again, in the Philippines, dances like the traditional Malay "tinikling" or heron dance not only draw their inspiration from the wild but would be inconceivable without the dramatic clashing of bamboo poles.

While it is easy to describe qualitatively the contributions of wild plants and animals, it is less easy to quantify them. Where wildlife supplies raw materials (as in timber and fish production), and where commercial transactions are adequately recorded, the contribution to gross national product is relatively simple to assess. This is not so where the contributions are genetic or in the form of ecological support.

Some contributions can be evaluated theoretically by calculating the replacement costs. What, for example, would it cost farmers to spray the rice crop to protect it from grassy stunt virus, if they did not have the resistance conferred by wild rice (Oryza nivara)? Or how much would it cost in terms of flood control, disaster relief and harbour dredging, if natural forests were not protecting a watershed?

Such methods are not entirely satisfactory. They yield results that are somewhat speculative and are not strictly comparable with corresponding evaluations of wildlife's contribution of raw materials. Furthermore, they ignore the question of capacity to pay. Before farmers had rice cultivars resistant to grassy stunt virus they could not afford to spray more, so they simply lost their crop. Loss of natural watershed protection or other ecological support generally leads not only to greater costs but also to greater vulnerability of the poor, who cannot bear current costs let alone increased ones.

Even the apparently straightforward task of quantifying the value of raw materials from the wild can produce misleading results. A pharmacological compound can only be old for so much, yet there may be no substitute for it in the treatment of a particular disease. Its market value therefore represents only a part of its true value to the health service or to society as a whole. There is also a great deal of economic activity in developing countries that goes unmeasured by statisticians. Much of the wildlife used for food, fuel and fibre is collected by the user (or his or her family). Even when wildlife is sold or exchanged it is done informally, without receipts and other documentation indispensable for the compilation of accurate statistics.

Wild plants and animals make their greatest contribution to human survival and wellbeing precisely in those poor rural economies where their use is usually grossly underestimated. One measure of the importance of wildlife to rural economies is the persistence of trade in species protected (on paper at least) by international and national law. In Bolivia, for example, the export of the skins of spotted cats and otters is illegal (the animals being on Appendix I of CITES, the Convention on International Trade in Endangered Species of Wild Flora and Fauna, to which Bolivia is a party). Yet the trade continues because it is so lucrative: the $500 a hunter can get for a jaguar skin easily exceeds a year's income from farming (Freeman et al 1980).

A related measure is the rapid depletion of many wild resources - evidence that demand is quickly outstripping supply. In some countries the need for firewood is so acute that the land has been denuded of trees and shrubs over wide areas. Around one fishing centre in the African Sahel, where wood is the fuel used in fish drying, deforestation extends as far away as 100 kilometres (62 miles)(FAO 1978c). In Mali firewood is so scarce that its cost has risen by 15% every year for the past seven years: even in the well-watered south the nearest wood is a two hour walk from any village of 1,500 people; in the arid north it is 50 kilometres (31 miles) away (Arid Lands Information Center 1980b).

Heavy pressure such as this threatens wild genetic resources in several parts of the world. Wild fruit and nut trees in West Asia are being felled for fuel and timber, and wild olives in Algeria and Niger are at risk because of overgrazing and browsing by cattle and goats and overcutting for fodder (Prescott-Allen and Prescott-Allen 1981). Overexploitation (for home consumption and for trade) threatens almost 40% of all animal species known to be in danger of extinction and is the most serious of the threats faced by reptiles (IUCN 1980).

Overexploitation is exceeded in its impact on wildlife only by habitat destruction. It is unquestionably the biggest threat to the survival of both plant and animal species, and of valuable genotypes within species. Almost 70% of the animal species facing extinction are threatened by habitat alteration or loss (IUCN 1980). (The figures of almost 70% for habitat destruction and almost 40% for overexploitation add up to more than 100% because many species are theatened by both.)

On land, tropical forests are being felled and burned for shifting agriculture, spontaneous settlement, government colonisation schemes, clearance for plantations and ranches, fuelwood cutting, and logging.

Gambia's forest area was reduced by 30% between 1958 and 1973 (Arid Lands Information Center 1981); and in Liberia, where the rotation rate of shifting agriculture in the more heavily populated areas has dropped from 15-25 years to 2-4 years, an estimated 30,000 hectares (74,000 acres) are degraded or transformed to scrub every year (Library of Congress 1980d).

At sea and in the coastal zone, wetlands, coral reefs and other nutrient sources and nurseries of fisheries are succumbing to pollution, "reclamation" and other forms of degradation. Along the coasts of Pakistan, India and Sri Lanka productive lagoons are becoming clogged with silt from erosion inland, mangroves are being stripped for fuelwood, and estuaries are being affected by agricultural and industrial pollutants (Salm 1981). On balance, the only habitats that are increasing are built-up areas and degraded land.

Habitat destruction not only threatens the survival of species; it also threatens the wellbeing of human communities that depend on wildlife for income or some other good. A large number of wild medicinal plants are considered at risk because of loss of habitat in Sri Lanka (Pinto 1978), Nepal (Saiju 1978) and Vietnam (Agarwal 1978). The rattan resource in Southeast Asia is being rapidly depleted by the conversion of large tracts of forest to agriculture and settlement, particularly the more accessible forests (Menon 1980).

Wild genetic resources are also affected. With the expansion of agriculture, urbanisation and other incompatible land uses, populations of wild species shrink and disappear.

* In South America certain stands of wild tomatoes known 20 to 25 years ago no longer exist, due to destruction of their habitats by land clearance for farms, industry and houses (Rick 1977).

* Large areas of wild cocoa habitat in Colombia, Ecuador and Peru have been devasted first by petroleum exploration and exploitation and subsequently by colonisation schemes (Chalmers 1972; Soria 1975).

* In Southeast Asia logging operations and expansion of cultivation are reducing the habitats of wild bananas and sugarcane (Daniels et al 1975; Valmayor 1979).

* Agriculture is constricting the habitats of wild wheats in West Asia and wild coffee in Africa (Committee on Genetic Vulnerability of Major Crops, Agricultural Board 1972; IBPGR 1980; Mengesha 1975).

Many more crop relatives may prove to be at risk, particularly species with restricted distributions occurring in areas where habitat destruction is pronounced - tropical forests, heavily populated mountain regions, and arid lands subject to desertification. Among the kinds of plants found in such areas and most likely to be threatened are mangoes, cottons, breadfruits, coffees, citrus, tomatoes and potatoes (Prescott-Allen and Prescott-Allen 1981).

Because genetic variation is not distributed evenly in a species it is possible for valuable genotypes to be threatened even though the species is abundant.

* Wild rice (Oryza nivara) is a widespread weed in south and southeast Asia, China and northern Australia, yet only one sample from central India is resistant to grassy stunt virus.

* The owl monkey (Aotus trivirgatus) is widely distributed throughout Central and South America, but it is the rare and dwindling northern Colombian subspecies that is valuable for human malaria research (Interagency Primate Steering Committee 1978).

* The hoop pine (Araucaria cunninghamii) is indigenous to New Guinea and northeastern Australia. As a species it is not threatened, but several populations in New Guinea are. New Guinea provenances are both more productive and better adapted to other tropical countries than are provenances from Australia (FAO 1981c).

The main conclusions of this report are:

* First, wildlife makes an important, and often an essential, contribution to local and national economies of developing countries.

* Second, much of this contribution is difficult to evaluate, and readily overlooked, because it is part of the hidden economy of rural areas, informal markets or illegal trade channels.

* Third, while wild resources should be conserved and developed sustainably, many are either overexploited or depleted by habitat loss.

* Fourth, concern for threatened species can induce a false sense of security. Sometimes the species is not at risk, but valuable genotypes or other subdivisions of the species are.

How can we best maintain and sustainably develop wildlife as a resource, and reconcile it with other development needs? The World Conservation Strategy (IUCN 1980) proposed three main steps:

* National and regional evaluations of the contributions of wildlife

* Conservation of wild resources

* Integration of conservation with development

The information available on the contribution of wildlife to local and national economies, and on the ways in which the wildlife resource is threatened, is not sufficient for effective national action. The knowledge that the resource is sufficiently important and sufficiently at risk to justify detailed evaluation is no substitute for that evaluation. The conservation and sustainable development of wild resources involve difficult decisions. The more precise and comprehensive the information, the easier those decisions will be, and the more rational and effective will be the planning, allocation and management of competing uses.

There should be national evaluations of the economic importance and management problems of wild living resources, and regional evaluations for groups of smaller nations such as the islands of the Pacific and the Caribbean.

The second main step is the conservation of wild resources. This requires a tripartite approach consisting of ex situ protection, in situ protection, and rational planning, allocation and management of resource use.

Ex situ protection means the maintenance of resources in gene banks, zoos, botanical gardens, farms and plantations. It is the chief and generally the only practical means of maintaining the germplasm of domesticated plants and animals. But it is also an important supplementary means of safeguarding wild genetic resources. Its scope is greatest with plants, since with some exceptions they are easier to maintain ex situ than are most animals. However, the conservation of wild animals in captivity is sometimes the only way of ensuring their survival, particularly if their habitats are being severely reduced.

In situ protection means the maintenance of resources in national parks, nature reserves and other protected areas. It is the chief means of maintaining wild plant and animal genetic resources. It can also help conserve areas that are important for ecological support, such as watershed forests and critical habitats. Protected areas serve many other valuable functions, well exemplified by the biosphere reserves of Unesco's Man and the Biosphere (MAB) programme. Major objectives of biosphere reserves are conservation, research, education and training; they can combine maintenance of ecosystems and of wild genetic resources with the advancement of ecological knowledge and the improvement of biological management skills.

A weakness of current systems of in situ protection is that they are largely oriented towards species and ecosystem conservation and hardly at all towards the conservation of genotypes. Species conservation aims to maintain a sufficient number of viable populations of a species to minimise the chance of that species' extinction. Ecosystem conservation aims to maintain as comprehensive a sample as possible of representative and unique ecosystems. But neither will necessarily be concerned with maintaining the amount of genetic variation within species that users of genetic resources need to have available.

To preserve wild genetic resources, protected areas need to be designed, distributed and managed so that they maintain as much diversity as possible: clinal, interpopulational and intra-populational. While in situ and ex situ protection are essential for the conservation of genetic resources they are not sufficient; management is needed as well. The genetic resources needed for development are so widespread and diverse that genebanks and protected areas alone are not equal to the task of maintaining them all.

The sustainable use of the wildlife that contributes directly to the supply of food, fuel, fibre, medicines and other goods depends not only on regulation of exploitation but also on the maintenance of the habitats of the species concerned. Often, these habitats are ubiquitous, and beyond the scope of reserves to protect them unaided. Countries must soundly plan, allocate and manage land and water so as to achieve a sustainable combination of development on the one hand and of maintenance of the biological resources required for development on the other.

The third step necessary to maintain and develop the wildlife resource is to increase the utility of the biosphere. Many development decisions, however, focus so narrowly on increasing this utility that they overlook the concomitant need to maintain the biosphere's capacity to be useful. The World Conservation Strategy recommends several measures to overcome this problem.

* First, governments should have an explicit policy for the conservation of living resources, a policy that is cross-sectoral (applying to all sectors that depend on or have an impact on living resources) and concerned as much with maintenance as with production. One way of achieving this is through the inclusion of a conservation chapter in the national economic development plan or equivalent.

* Second, they should articulate a strategy for implementing the conservation policy.

* Third, environmental planning needs to be greatly improved and land and water uses allocated on the basis of that improved planning.

The rationale of these measures is a simple one. Development is production; and conservation is the maintenance of the means of production. Both are necessary for human survival and wellbeing.

The earlier in the decision-making process that potential conflicts and compatibilities between conservation and development are addressed, the easier it will be to resolve the conflicts and take advantage of the compatibilities, and the cheaper and more effective for society the decision-making process will be.

The conservation of wildlife is sometimes presented as being at best irrelevant, at worst an obstacle to development. In this report we have tried to show that it is neither. On the contrary, wildlife's actual and potential contributions to economic and social development are substantial.

By conserving and using their wild resources sustainably, developing countries have much to gain. The rich world also has much to gain by assisting them to do this. Many of the products it imports come from the wild plants and animals of developing countries. Several valuable crops grown in the North - tomato, tobacco, and sugarcane, for example - could not be grown at all without the disease resistance provided by their wild relatives from the South.

The conservation of wildlife is a contribution to the prosperity of all peoples and all nations, developing and developed.

84

REFERENCES

Adamson, A.D. 1971. Oleoresins: production and markets with particular reference to the United Kingdom. Tropical Products Institute G56. 46pp.

Adamson, A.D. & J.-M.K. Bell. 1974. The market for gum arabic. Tropical Products Institute G87. 99pp.

Agarwal, A. 1978. Drugs and the Third World. Earthscan, International Institute for Environment and Development. 70 pp.

Ajayi, S.S. 1979. Utilization of forest wildlife in West Africa. FAO. Rome. FO:MISC/79/26. 76 pp.

Almeyda, N. & F.W. Martin. 1976. Cultivation of neglected tropical fruits with promise. Part I. The mangosteen. USDA. ARS. ARS-S-155. 18 pp.

Anonymous. 1981. The fished-out gulf of Thailand: years of greed and dynamite - and a nearly dead sea. Time. February 23:53.

Aoyama, T. 1973. The South China Sea fisheries: demersal resources. South China Sea Fisheries Development and Coordinating Programme. FAO. UNDP. Rome. SCS/DEV/73/3. 80 pp.

Applezweig, N. 1977. Dioscorea - the pill crop. In: D.S. Seigler (editor). Crop resources: 149-163.

Arid Lands Information Center. 1980a. Draft environmental profile on Upper Volta. Office of Arid Land Studies. University of Arizona. Tucson. 138 pp.

Arid Lands Information Center. 1980b. Draft environmental profile on Mali. Office of Arid Lands Studies. University of Arizona. Tucson. 69 pp.

Arid Lands Information Center. 1981. Draft environmental profile on the Gambia. Office of Arid Lands Studies. University of Arizona. Tucson. 85 pp.

Arnold, J.E.M. & J. Jongma. 1978. Fuelwood and charcoal in developing countries. Unasylva 29(118): 2-9.

Asibey, E.O.A. 1974. Wildlife as a source of protein in Africa south of the Sahara. Biological Conservation 6(1): 32-39.

Basson, P.W., J.E. Burchard, Jr, J.T. Hardy & A.R.G. Price. 1977. Biotopes of the western Arabian Gulf: marine life and environments of Saudi Arabia. Aramco Department of Loss Prevention and Environmental Affairs. Dhahran, Saudi Arabia. 284 pp.

Bogdan, A.V. 1977. Tropical pasture and fodder plants (grasses and legumes). Longman. London, New York. 475 pp.

Brennan, J. 1981. The original Thai cookbook. Richard Marek Publishers Inc. New York. 318 pp.

Brokaw, H.P. (editor). 1978. Wildlife and America: Contributions to an understanding of American wildlife and its conservation. Council on Environmental Quality, US Fish and Wildlife Service, US Forest Service, National Oceanic and Atmospheric Administration. Washington, DC. 532 pp.

Butynski, T.M. & W. von Richter. 1974. In Botswana most of the meat is wild. Unasylva 26(106): 24-29.

Chalmers, W.S. 1972. The conservation of wild cacao populations: the plant breeder's most urgent task. 4th International Cocoa Conference. January 1972. Trinidad and Tobago.

Chapman, V.J. 1970. Seaweeds and their uses. Methuen & Co. Ltd. London. 304 pp.

Ch'en, W.-C. 1977. Introductory remarks to the WHO seminar on the use of medicinal plants in health care. In WHO. Final report: seminar on the use of medicinal plants in health care: 139-143.

Chou, C.-C. 1977. The significance of using Chinese materia medica in medical and health work. In WHO. Final report: seminar on the use of medicinal plants in health care: 85-93

Chou, H.-C. 1977. How we promote the utilisation of plant medicine by health organisations at the basic levels in China. In WHO. Final report: seminar on the use of medicinal plants in health care: 95-99.

Collins, J.L. 1960. The pineapple: botany, cultivation and utilization. Leonard Hill (Books) Limited. London. Interscience Publishers Inc. New York. 294 pp. J.L. Collins, Pineapple Research Institute, Honolulu, Hawaii.

Committee on Genetic Vulnerability of Major Crops, Agricultural Board. 1972. Genetic vulnerability of major crops. Academy of Sciences. Washington, DC. 307 pp.

Coppen, J.J.W. 1979. Steroids: from plants to pills - the changing picture. Tropical Science 21(3): 125-141.

Corner, E.J.H. 1966. The natural history of palms. Weidenfeld and Nicolson. London. Coursey, D.G. 1967. Yams: an account of the nature, origins, cultivation and utilization of the useful memebers of the Dioscoreaceae. Longmans, Green and Co. Ltd. London 230 pp.

Coursey, D.G. 1967. <u>Yams: an account of the nature, origins, cultivation and utilization of the useful members of the Dioscoreaceae</u>. Longmans, Green and Co Ltd. London. 230 pp.

Daniels, J., P. Smith & N. Paton. 1975. The origin of sugarcanes and centres of genetic diversity in <u>Saccharum</u>. In J.T. Williams, C.H. Lamoureux N. Wulijarni-Soetjipto (editors).

Das, D.C. 1977. Soil conservation practices and erosion control in India: a case study. In <u>Soil conservation and management in developing countries</u>. FAO report of an expert consultation. 22-26 November 1976. Rome. <u>FAO Soils Bulletin 33</u>.

Davidson, A. 1975. <u>Fish and fish dishes of Laos</u>. Charles E. Tuttle Co Inc. Rutland & Tokyo. 206 pp.

Davy, F.B. & A. Chouinard (editors). 1981. <u>Induced fish breeding in Southeast Asia</u>. Report of a workshop held in Singapore. 25-28 November 1980. IDRC-178e. 48 pp.

Dransfield, J. 1979a. <u>A manual of the rattans of the Malay Peninsula</u>. Forest Department. Ministry of Primary Industries. Malaysia. 270 pp.

Dransfield, J. 1979b. <u>Report of consultancy on rattan development carried out in Thailand, Philippines, Indonesia and Malaysia</u>. 14 March-8 May 1979. For FAO Regional Office for Asia and the Far East. Bangkok. 40 pp.

Duke, J.A. 1981. <u>Handbook of legumes of world economic importance</u>. Plenum Press. New York, London. 345 pp.

Eckholm, E.P. 1975. The other energy crisis: firewood. <u>Worldwatch Paper 1</u>. Worldwatch Institute. 22 pp.

Eckholm, E.P. 1979. Forest renewal in India. <u>Natural History</u> 88(6): 12-27.

Erfurth, T. 1974. International trade and trade flows of tropical forest products. In: FAO. <u>Properties, uses and marketing of tropical timber. Volume 2</u>: 99-107.

Erfurth, T. & H. Rusche. 1976a. <u>The marketing of tropical wood</u>. A. Wood species from African tropical moist forests. FAO Forestry Department. 60 pp.

Erfurth, T. & H. Rusche. 1976b. <u>The marketing of tropical wood</u>. B. Wood species from South American tropical moist forests. FAO Forestry Department.

Fairbairn, J.W. 1976. New plant sources of opiates. <u>Planta Medica</u> 29(1): 26-31.

FAO. 1974. <u>Properties, uses and marketing of tropical timber. Volume 2 - meeting papers</u>. FO: MISC/74/7. 236 pp.

FAO. 1975. <u>Report on a pilot study on the methodology of conservation of forest genetic resources</u>. FAO. Rome. FO:MISC/75/8. 127 pp.

FAO. 1976. <u>Appendixes</u>. Extracted from: The marketing of tropical wood. C. Wood species from Southeast Asian tropical moist forests. FAO Forestry Department. FO:MISC/76/8.

FAO. 1977a. <u>Provisional food balance sheets: 1972-74 average</u>. FAO. Rome

FAO. 1977b. <u>1976 yearbook of forest products</u>.

FAO. 1978a. <u>Review of the state of world fishery resources</u>. 12th Session. Committee on Fisheries. 12-16 June 1978. Rome. COFI/78/Inf.4.

FAO. 1978b. <u>Fishery commodity situation and outlook</u>. 12th Session. Committee on Fisheries. 12-17 June 1978. Rome. COFI/78/Inf.5.

FAO. 1978c. <u>The state of food and agriculture 1977</u>. FAO. Rome.

FAO. 1978d. Forestry for local community development. <u>FAO Forestry Paper 7</u>. 114 pp.

FAO. 1980a. <u>Production, consumption and trade of minor meats - trends, prospects and development issues</u>. Committee on Commodity Problems: Intergovernmental Group on Meat. Ninth Session. 8-12 December 1980. Rome. 8 pp.

FAO. 1980b. <u>1979 yearbook of fishery statistics: catches and landings</u>. Vol 48. FAO Fisheries Series. 384 pp.

FAO. 1980c. 1979 FAO production yearbook. Volume 33. <u>FAO Statistics Series No 4 28</u>. 309 pp.

FAO. 1980d. 1979 FAO trade yearbook. <u>FAO Statistics Series No 29</u>. 357 pp.

FAO. 1980e. <u>1979 yearbook of fishery statistics: fishery commodities</u>.

FAO. 1981a. Commodity review and outlook: 1980-81. <u>FAO Economic and Social Development Series No 20</u>. 120 pp.

FAO. 1981b. <u>1979 yearbook of forest products</u>.

FAO. 1981c. <u>Data book on endangered forest tree species and provenances</u>. Rome. FO:MISC/81/11. 64 pp.

86

Farnsworth, N.R. 1969a. Drugs from higher plants. Tile & Till 55(2): 32-36.

Farnsworth, N.R. 1969b. Drugs from animals. Tile & Till 55(4): 67-71.

Farnsworth, N.R. 1977. The current importance of plants as a source of drugs. In D.S. Seigler (editor). Crop resources: 61-73.

Ferwerda, F.P. & F. Wit (editors). 1969. Outlines of perennial crop breeding in the tropics. Miscellaneous Papers 4. H. Veenman and Zonen, N.V. Wageningen. 511 pp.

Frankel, O.H. & J.G. Hawkes (editors). 1975. Crop genetic resources for today and tomorrow. International Biological Programme 2. Cambridge University Press. Cambridge, London, New York, Melbourne. 492 pp.

Free, J.B. 1970. Insect pollination of crop plants. Academic Press. London, New York. 544 pp.

Freeman, P.H., B. Cross, R.D. Flannery, D.A. Harcharik, G.S. Hartshorn, G. Simmonds & J.D. Williams. 1980. Bolivia: state of the environment and natural resources: a field study. JRB Associates, Inc. McLean, Virginia.

Glicksman, M. & R.E. Sand. 1973. Gum arabic. In R.L. Whistler & J.N. BeMiller (editors). Industrial gums: polysaccharides and their derivatives: 197-263.

Goldstein, A.M. & E.N. Alter. 1973. Gum karaya. In R.L. Whistler & J.N. BeMiller (editors). Industrial gums: polysaccharides and their derivatives: 273-287.

Government of India. 1980. Sixth five year plan. New Delhi.

Grubben, G.J.H. 1977. Tropical vegetables and their genetic resources. IBPGR. Rome. AGPE:IBPGR/77/23. 197 pp.

Guldager, P. 1975. Ex situ conservation stands in the tropics. In FAO. Report on a pilot study on the methodology of conservation of forest genetic resources: 85-92.

Gupta, R. 1981. Genetic resources of medicinal plants in a world prospective. FAO/UNEP/IBPGR Technical Conference on Crop Genetic Resources. 6-10 April 1981. Rome. 28 pp.

Hahn, S.K., A.K. Howland & E.R. Terry. 1973. Cassava breeding at IITA. Proceedings of the 3rd Symposium of the International Society for Tropical Root Crops. 2-9 December 1973: 4-10.

Hanlon, J. 1979. When the scientist meets the medicine men. Nature 279: 284-285.

Harlan, J.R. 1976. Genetic resources in wild relatives of crops. Crop Science 16: 329-333.

Hathway, D.E. 1959. Myrobalans: an important tanning material. Tropical Science 1: 85-106.

Hawkes, J.G. 1958. Significance of wild species and primitive forms for potato breeding. Euphytica 7: 257-270.

IBPGR. 1980. Report of a meeting of a working group on coffee. 11-13 December 1979. Rome.

IDRC. 1980. Rattan: a report of a workshop held in Singapore. 4-6 June 1979. IDRC-155e. 76 pp.

Imle, E.P. 1978. Hevea rubber - past and future. Economic Botany 32: 264-277.

Inskipp, T. & S. Wells. 1979. International trade in wildlife. Earthscan, International Institute for Environment and Development, Fauna Preservation Society. 104 pp.

Interagency Primate Steering Committee. 1978. National primate plan. US Department of Health, Education, and Welfare Publication (NIH) 80-1520. 81 pp.

International Trade Centre. 1979. International trade in tropical aquarium fish. ITC. Geneva. 137 pp.

IRRI Cropping Systems Program. 1973. 1973 annual report. IRRI.

IRRI. 1979. Brown planthopper: threat to rice production in Asia. IRRI. 369 pp.

IUCN. 1979. Red data book. Volume 3. Amphibia and Reptilia. IUCN, Unesco, UNEP, WWF.

IUCN. 1980. World conservation strategy. IUCN, UNEP, WWF. Gland and Nairobi.

Jennings, D.L. 1976. Cassava. In N.W. Simmonds (editor). Evolution of crop plants: 81-84.

Jolly, M.S. 1980. Distribution and differentiation in Antheraea species (Saturniidae: Lepidoptera). Paper presented in the XVI International Congress of Entomology. 3-9 August 1980. Kyoto, Japan. 18 pp.

Jolly, M.S., S.K. Sen & M.G. Das. 1976. Silk from the forest. Unasylva 28(114): 20-23.

Khush, G.S. 1978. Breeding methods and procedures employed at IRRI for developing rice germplasm with multiple resistance to diseases and insects. Tropical Agriculture Research Series No. 11: 69-76.

Khush, G.S. 1979. Genetics of and breeding for resistance to the brown planthopper. In IRRI. Brown planthopper: threat to rice production in Asia: 321-332

Khush, G.S., K.C. Ling, R.C. Aquino & V.M. Aguiero. 1977. Breeding for resistance to grassy stunt in rice. Plant Breeding Papers 1(4b):3-9.

King, F.W. 1978. The wildlife trade. In H.P. Brokaw (editor). Wildlife and America: contributions to an understanding of American wildlife and its conservation: 253-271.

Krostitz, W. 1979. The new international market for game meat. Unasylva 31(123): 32-36.

Kume, S. 1973. The south China Sea fisheries: tuna resources. South China Sea Fisheries Development and Coordinating Programme. FAO. UNDP. Rome. SCS/DEV/73/4. 18 pp.

Lessard, G. & A. Chouinard (editors). 1980. Bamboo research in Asia. Proceedings of a workshop held in Singapore. 28-30 May 1980. IDRC-159e. 228 pp.

Lewis, W.H. & M.P.F. Elvin-Lewis. 1977. Medical botany: plants affecting man's health. John Wiley & Sons. New York, London, Sydney, Toronto. 515 pp.

Library of Congress. 1979a. Draft environmental profile on Haiti. Library of Congress. Science and Technology Division. Washington, DC.

Library of Congress. 1979b. Draft environmental report on Guatemala. Library of Congress. Science and Technology Division. Washington, DC.

Library of Congress. 1979c. Draft environmental report on Nepal. Library of Congress. Science and Technology Division. Washington, DC. 54 pp.

Library of Congress. 1979d. Draft environmental report on Peru. Library of Congress. Science and Technology Division. Washington, DC.

Library of Congress. 1980a. Draft environmental profile on Bangladesh. Library of Congress. Science and Technology Division. Washington, DC. 98 pp.

Library of Congress. 1980b. Draft environmental report on India. Library of Congress. Science and Technology Division. Washington, DC. 161 pp.

Library of Congress. 1980c. Draft environmental report on the Philippines. Library of Congress. Science and Technology Division. Washington, DC.

Library of Congress. 1980d. Phase 1: environmental profile of Liberia. Library of Congress. Science and Technology Division. Washington, DC.

Lowe-McConnell, R.H. 1977. Ecology of fishes in tropical waters. The Institute of Biology's Studies in Biology No. 76. Edward Arnold (Publishers) Ltd. London. 64 pp.

MacNae, W. 1974. Mangrove forests and fisheries. FAO, UNDP. Rome. IOFC/DEV/74/34. 35 pp.

Maggs, D.H. 1972. Pistachios in Iran and California. Plant Introduction Review 9(1): 12-16.

Majid, A. & A. Hendranata. 1975. Selection and conservation problems in Hevea with special reference to Indonesia. In J.T. Williams, C.H. Lamoureux & N. Wulijarni-Soetjipto (editors). South East Asian plant genetic resources: 171-177.

Manning, C.E.F. 1969. The market for steroid drug precursors with particular reference to diosgenin. Tropical Products Institute Report G41. 20 pp.

McNeely, W.H. & D.J. Pettitt. 1973. Algin. In R.L. Whistler & J.N. BeMiller (editors). Industrial gums: polysaccharides and their derivatives: 49-81.

Menasveta, D., S. Shindo & S. Chullasorn. 1973. The South China Sea Fisheries: pelagic resources. South China Sea Fisheries Development and Coordinating Programme. FAO. UNDP. Rome. SCS/DEV/73/6. 68 pp.

Menon, K.D. 1980. Rattan: a state-of-the-art review. In IDRC. Rattan: a report of a workshop held in Singapore: 13-74.

Morton, J.F. 1977. Major medicinal plants: botany, culture and uses. Charles C. Thomas. Springfield, Illinois. 431 pp.

Moss, J.P. 1980. Wild species in the improvement of groundnuts.In R.J. Summerfield & A.H. Bunting (editors). Advances in legume science: 525-535.

Nakajima, H. 1977. Alternative approach for the use of medicinal plants in health care. In WHO. Final report: seminar on the use of medicinal plants in health care: 47-55.

National Academy of Sciencies. 1975. Underexploited tropical plants with promising economic value. NAS. Washington, DC. 188 pp.

National Academy of Sciences. 1979. Staff summary report: NAS participation in second Caribbean Commonwealth meeting on utilization of natural products. 22-27 April 1979. Port-of- Spain. 66 pp.

Naylor, J. 1976. Production, trade and utilisation of seaweeds and seaweed products. _FAO Fisheries Technical Paper No. 159_. FAO. Rome. FIPP/T159. 73 pp.

Obeid, M. & A.S. el Din. 1970. Ecological studies of the vegetation of the Sudan. I. Acacia senegal (L.) Willd and its natural regeneration. _Journal of Applied Ecology_ 7: 507-518.

Olmo, H.P. 1976. Grapes. In N.W. Simmonds (editor). _Evolution of crop plants_: 294-298.

Oomen, H.A.P.C. & G.J.H. Grubben. 1978. _Tropical leaf vegetables in human nutrition_. Department of Agricultural Research Communication 69. Koninklijk Instituut voor de Tropen. Amsterdam. 140 pp.

Openshaw, K. 1971. Present consumption and future requirements of wood in Tanzania. FO-SF/TAN 15. _FAO Technical Report 3_.

Penso, G. 1978. _Inventory of medicinal plants and compilation of a list of the most widely used plants_. Meeting on selection and characterisation of medicinal plants (vegetable drugs). 9-13 October 1978 Geneva, Switzerland. WHO. DPM/WP/78.2. 39 pp.

Penso, G. 1980. _Inventory of medicinal plants used in difference countries_. WHO. DPM/80.3. 724 pp.

Pereira, H.C. 1973. _Land use and water resources in temperate and tropical climates_. Cambridge University Press.

Phillips, L.L. 1976. Cotton. In N.W. Simmonds (editor). _Evolution of crop plants_: 196-200.

Pinto, M.E.R. 1978. _A review of the crop genetic resources of some important plants in Sri Lanka_. Report of IBPGR Workshop on South Asian Plant Genetic Resources. IBPGR, Rome. AGPE:IBPGR/78/17: 51-5

Polsena, P.P. 1977. Traditional medicine in the Lao People's Democratic Republic. In WHO. _Final report: seminar on the use of medicinal plants in health care_: 145-154.

Prescott-Allen, R. & C. Prescott-Allen. 1981. _In situ conservation of crop genetic resources_. A report to the International Board for Plant Genetic Resources.

Purseglove, J.W., E.G. Brown, C.L. Green & S.R.J. Robbins. 1981a._Spices. Volume 1_. Longman. London, New York. 439 pp.

Purseglove, J.W., E.G. Brown, C.L. Green & S.R.J. Robbins. 1981b. _Spices. Volume 2_. Longman. London, New York. 447-812 pp.

Ricciuti, E.R. 1980. The ivory wars. _Animal Kingdom_ 83(1): 6-59.

Rick, C.M. 1973. Potential genetic resources in tomato species: clues from observations in native habitats. In A.M. Srb (editor). _Basic life sciences. Volume 2_: 255-269.

Rick, C.M. 1976. Natural variability in wild species of _Lycopersicon_ and its bearing on tomato breeding. _Genetica Agraria_ 30: 249-259.

Rick, C.M. 1977. Conservation of tomato species germplasm. _California Agriculture_ 31: 32-33.

Rick, C.M. 1979. Potential improvement of tomatoes by controlled introgression of genes from wild species. In A.C. Zeven & A.M. van Harten (editors). _Proceedings of a conference broadening the genetic base of crops_: 167-173.

Rick, C.M. & P.G. Smith. 1953. Novel variations in tomato species hybrids. _American Naturalist_ 87: 359-373.

Robbins, S.R.J. & W.S.A. Matthews. 1974. Minor forest products. _Unasylva_ 26(106): 7-14.

Roet, E.C., D.S. Mack & N. Duplaix. 1981. _Psittacines imported by the United States (October 1979-June 1980)_. Proceedings of the ICBP Parrot Workshop. 15-19 April 1980. St. Lucia. Special report 7. 70 pp.

Rowe, P.R. & D.L. Richardson. 1975. Breeding bananas for disease resistance, fruit quality and yield. Tropical Agriculture Research Services (SIATSA). La Lima, Honduras. _Bulletin No. 2_. 41 pp.

Ruddle, K., D. Johnson, P.K. Townsend & J.D. Rees. 1978. _Palm sago: a tropical starch from marginal lands_. The University Press of Hawaii. Honolulu. 207 pp.

Rush, D.W. & E. Epstein. 1976. Genotypic responses to salinity: differences between salt-sensitive and salt-tolerant genotypes of the tomato. _Plant Physiology_ 57: 162-166.

Saiju, H.K. 1978. _Annex: germplasm of medicinal plants in Nepal_. Report of IBPGR Workshop on South Asian Plant Genetic Resources. IBPGR. Rome. AGPE:IBPGR/78/17: 46-49.

Sakamoto, S. 1976. Breeding of a new sweet potato variety, Minamiyutaka, by the use of wild relatives. _JARQ_ 10(4): 183-186.

Sale, J.B. Unpublished. _Report on the importance and values of wild plants and animals in Africa_. Part I. Prepared for IUCN, Gland.

Salm, R.V. 1981. _Critical marine habitats in Pakistan, western India and Sri Lanka_. US Fish and Wildlife Service. Washington, DC.

Schery, R.W. 1972. *Plants for man*. 2nd edition. Prentice-Hall, Inc. Englewood Cliffs, New Jersey. 657 pp.

Seigler, D.S. (editor). 1977. *Crop resources*. Proceedings of the 17th Annual Meeting of the Society for Economic Botany. 13-17 June 1976. Urbana, Illinois. Academic Press, Inc. New York, San Francisco, London. 233 pp.

Selby, H.H. & W.H. Wynne. 1973. Agar. In R.L. Whistler & J.N. BeMiller (editors). *Industrial gums: polysaccharides and their derivatives*: 29-48.

Shane, M. 1977. The economics of a sabah rattan industry. In W.W. Yen, & M. Shane (editors). *A Sabah rattan industry*: 43-53.

Sharma, L.C. 1978. *Development of forests and forest-based industries*. Bishen Singh Mahendra Pal Singh. Dehra Dun. 237 pp.

Sharma, Y.M.L. 1980. Bamboo in the Asia-Pacific region. In G. Lessard & A. Chouinard (editors). *Bamboo research in Asia*: 99-120.

Simmonds, N.W. (editor). 1976. *Evolution of crop plants*. Longman. London, New York. 339 pp.

Simmonds, N.W. 1979. *Principles of Crop Improvement*. Longman. London, New York. 408 pp.

Singh, M.P., S.B. Malla, S.B. Rajbhandari & A. Manandhar. 1979. Medicinal plants of Nepal - retrospects and prospects. *Economic Botany* 33(2): 185-198.

Smith, N.J.H. 1977. Human exploitation of terra firme fauna in Amazonia. *Ciencia e Cultura* 30(1): 17-23.

Somigliana, J.C. 1973. Sinopsis del estado economico actual y perspectivas del desenvolvimiento de la industria del "extracto (tanino) de quebrachos" de Argentina. *Revista Forestal Argentina* 17: 101-106.

Soria, J. 1975. Recent cocoa collecting expeditions. In O.H. Frankel & J.G. Hawkes (editors). *Crop genetic resources for today and tomorrow*: 175-179.

Srb, A.M. (editor). 1973. *Basic life sciences*. Volume 2. Plenum. New York.

Stalker, H.T. 1980. Utilisation of wild species for crop improvement. *Advances in Agronomy* 33: 111-147.

Summerfield, RJ. & A.H. Bunting (editors). 1980. *Advances in legume science*. Volume 1 of the Proceedings of the International Legume Conference. 31 July-4 August 1978. Kew. Royal Botanic Gardens. Kew. 667 pp.

Tapiador, D.D., H.F. Henderson, M.N. Delmendo & H. Tsutsui. 1977. Freshwater fisheries and aquaculture in China. *FAO Fisheries Technical Paper No. 168*. FIR/T168. FAO. Rome. 84 pp.

Towle, G.A. 1973. Carrageenan. In R.L. Whistler & J.N. BeMiller (editors). *Industrial gums: polysaccharides and their derivatives*: 83-114.

Toxopeus, H. 1969. Cacao. In F.P. Ferwerda & F. Wit (editors). *Outlines of perennial crop breeding in the tropics*: 79-109.

Tyler, V.E. 1979. Plight of plant-drug research in the United States today. *Economic Botany* 33(4): 377-383.

UNIDO. 1978. *Report of the technical consultation on production of drugs from medicinal plants in developing countries*. 13-20 March 1978. Lucknow, India. ID/222 (ID/WG.271/6). 45 pp.

USAID. 1979. *Environmental and natural resources management in developing countries: a report to Congress. Volume 1*. USAID. Department of State. Washington, DC.

USDA. 1976. Tree nuts. *USDA Foreign Agriculture Circular*. July. FN 5-76.

Valmayor, R.V. 1979. Banana and plantain collections in Indonesia. *Plant Genetic Resources Newsletter* 36:10-13.

Veblen, T.T. 1978. Guatemalan conifers. *Unasylva* 29(118): 25-32.

Vietmeyer, N. 1981. Man's new best friends. *Quest* Jan/Feb 5(1): 43-49.

Vohra, B.C. 1978. *Managing India's land and water resources*.

Vos, A. de. 1977. Game as food: a report on its significance in Africa and Latin America. *Unasylva* 29(116): 2-12.

Waard, P.W.F. de. 1980. Problem areas and prospects of production of pepper (Piper nigrum L.): an overview. Royal Tropical Institute, Amsterdam. *Department of Agricultural Research Bulletin 308*. 29 pp.

Welcomme, R.L. 1974. Some general and theoretical considerations on the fish production of African rivers. *CIFA Occasional Paper No. 3*. CIFA/OP 3. FAO. Rome. 26 pp.

Welcomme, R.L. 1975. The fisheries ecology of African   floodplains. CIFA Technical Paper No. 3. CIFA/T3
    FAO. Rome. 51   pp.

Werkhoven, J. & J.G. Ohler. 1968. Babassu. Tropical Abstracts 23(12).

Whistler, R.L. & J.N. BeMiller (editors). 1973. Industrial gums: polysaccharides and their derivatives.
    2nd edition. Academic   Press. New York, San Francisco, London. 807 pp.

Whitmore, T.C. (editor) 1973. Tree flora of Malaya: a manual for foresters. Volume 2. Longman. 444 pp.

WHO. 1977. Final report: seminar on the use of medicinal plants in health care. 13-17 September 1977.
    Tokyo, Japan. Regional   Office for the Western Pacific. Manila, Philippines.   ICP/DPM/001. 179 pp.

WHO. 1979. The selection of essential drugs. Second Report of the WHO Expert Committee. WHO Technical
    Report Series 641. 44 pp. Willan, R.L. 1973. Forestry: improving the use of genetic   resources. Span
    16(3): 119-122.

Williams, J.T., C.H. Lamoureux & N. Wulijarni-Soetjipto   (editors). 1975. South   East   Asian plant
    genetic resources.   IBPGR, BIOTROP & LIPI. Bogor. 272 pp.

Woodroof, J.G. 1979. Tree nuts: production, processing, products. 2nd edition. AVI Publishing Company,
    Inc. Westport,   Connecticut. 731 pp.

Yen, W.W. & M. Shane (editors). 1977. A Sabah rattan industry. Transcript of meeting on prepolicy
    discussion on rattan in   Sabah. 23 July 1977. SAFODA. Kota Kinabalu, Sabah.

Zeven, A.C. & A.M. van Harten (editors). 1979. Proceedings of the conference broadening the genetic base
    of crops. 3-7 July 1978.   Wageningen, Netherlands. Pudoc. Wageningen. 347 pp.

EARTHSCAN PAPERBACKS

<u>A Village in a Million</u> by Sumi Krishna Chauhan (1979) English only. Price: £2.00/$5.00

<u>Mud, mud</u> - The potential of earth-based materials for Third World housing by Anil Agarwal (1981) English, French and Spanish. Price: £2.50/$5.50

<u>Water, Sanitation, Health - for All?</u> Prospects for the International Drinking Water Supply and Sanitation Decade, 1981-90 by Anil Agarwal, James Kimondo, Gloria Moreno and Jon Tinker (1981) English only. Price: £3.00/$5.50

<u>Carbon Dioxide, Climate and Man</u> by John Gribbin (1981) English only. Price: £2.50/$5.50

<u>Fuel Alcohol</u>: Energy and Environment in a Hungry World by Bill Kovarik (1982) English only. Price: £3.00/$5.50

<u>Stockholm Plus Ten</u>: Promises, Promises? The decade since the 1972 UN Environment Conference by Robin Clarke and Lloyd Timberlake (1982) English only. Price: £2.50/$5.50

<u>Tropical Moist Forests</u>: the resource, the people, the threat by Catherine Caufield (1982) English, French and Spanish. Price: £3.00/$5.50

<u>Desertification</u>: how people make deserts, how people can stop, and why they don´t by Alan Grainger (1982) English and French. Price: £3.00/$5.50

<u>Gasifiers: fuel for siege economies</u> by Gerald Foley, Geoffrey Barnard and Lloyd Timberlake (1983) English only. Price: £3.00/$5.50

<u>A million villages, a million Decades?</u> The World Water and Sanitation Decade from two South Indian villages by Sumi Krishna Chauhan and K. Gopalakrishnan (1983) English only. Price: £3.00/$5.50

<u>Who puts the water in the taps?</u> Community participation in Third World drinking water, sanitation and health by Sumi Krishna Chauhan et al (1984) English only. Price: £3.00/$5.50

<u>Stoves and trees</u> by Gerald Foley, Patricia Moss and Lloyd Timberlake (1984) English only. Price: £3.50/$5.50

<u>Fuelwood: the energy crisis that won´t go away</u> by Erik Eckholm, Gerald Foley, Geoffrey Barnard and Lloyd Timberlake (1984) English only. Price: £3.50/$5.50

<u>Natural disasters - Acts of God or acts of Man?</u> by Anders Wijkma and Lloyd Timberlake (1984) English and Spanish. £3.50/$5.50

<u>Urban land and shelter for the poor</u> by Patrick McAuslan (1985) English and Spanish. Price: £3.50/$5.50

<u>Africa in crisis</u>: the causes, the cures of environmental bankruptcy by Lloyd Timberlake (1985) English only. £3.95/$6.25

<u>Acid earth - the global threat of acid pollution</u> by John McCormick (1985) English only. £3.95/£6.25

<u>Waterlogged wealth - why waste the world's wet places?</u> by Edward Maltby (1986) English only. £3.95/$7.75

<u>Genes from the wild</u>

using wild genetic resources for food and raw materials

by Robert and Christine Prescott-Allen

Describes the growing contribution of wild genetic resources to the production of food and raw materials, describes their characteristics, explains the benefits and problems of using them, and outlines the threats posed and the measures being taken to conserve them. Numerous examples of the real and potential use of wild genetic resources are cited.

English only   (1983)   Price: £3.00/$5.50

All Earthscan publications are available from:

EARTHSCAN   EARTHSCAN WASHINGTON
3 Endsleigh Street   1717 Massachusetts Avenue NW
London WC1H ODD   Washington DC 20036
UK   USA